Letters to Polly

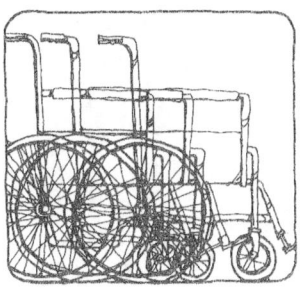

Letters to Polly
...on the Gift of Affliction

MELVIN E. SCHOONOVER

Wipf & Stock
PUBLISHERS
Eugene, Oregon

Wipf and Stock Publishers
199 W 8th Ave, Suite 3
Eugene, OR 97401

Letters to Polly
. . . on the Gift of Affliction
By Schoonover, Melvin
Copyright©1971 by Schoonover, Melvin
ISBN: 1-59752-892-7
Publication date 7/17/2006
Previously published by William B. Eerdmans Publishing Company, 1971

Contents

I.	Handicap	7
II.	Liberation	27
III.	Travel	47
IV.	Education	67
V.	Freedom	85

Handicap

1

Dear Polly

You are back in the hospital and have just had some more surgery. I suppose all parents suffer under such circumstances; the welfare of our children is our point of greatest vulnerability. Perhaps my suffering is more intense because two things happen to me when you are in pain—I relive my own childhood and I am reminded that I bear a peculiar responsibility for your suffering.

Even though I thought I was prepared for this hospitalization and this "elective" surgery, I have found that I really wasn't. The day I left you at the elevator, on your way to the operating room, crying, "Daddy, I'm scared," great rage welled up inside me—rage at the world, but most of all rage at myself. I drove uptown like a madman. Even I was scared at my reactions, and I feared that I might use the automobile in such a fashion as to bring harm to someone if not myself.

I have now decided to tackle the problem in another way. In the next few weeks, while you are in the hospital, I am going to write you a series of letters on my experiences and feelings about being a cripple. My hope is that, in what will doubtless be a painful exercise, I can come to terms with some of my own feelings, help you understand your very strange father a little better, and also help you come to terms with all kinds of problems and frustrations which you face increasingly.

The earliest memories I have are of pain and of separation from my family. The pain is associated with the broken bones I began to have at age two months; the separation with long stretches in James Whitcomb Riley Hospital in Indianapolis, more than a hundred miles from the Indiana farm where I lived as a child.

Pain. How does one understand or measure it? It is a part of nature's warning system that something is wrong with the body. It was because I began crying and wouldn't stop as my mother changed my diaper one day that a doctor was summoned and, in due course, it was established that I was the possessor of a rare malady known as *osteogenesis imperfecta.* For reasons still unknown, calcium is not properly laid down on my bones to make them hard and strong; instead they are thin and brittle, easy to break. To be sure, I did not have the worst possible case. At least I had not been born with multiple fractures, as some victims are, nor did I have trouble with skull or spinal fractures, which pose such an acute threat for others. Nevertheless, through the years I managed to break arms and legs, collar bones and scapulae more than fifty times, until the condition reached some kind of stability in adolescence.

Do the fractures of *osteogenesis imperfecta* patients hurt more than those experienced by other people? I don't know. I do know that many factors enter into pain. There is for us, perhaps, a certain kind of sensitivity because the broken bones can occur at any time from the most ridiculous causes. I once broke my femur, for example, while having a nightmare. And as you already perceive, the anticipation of being hurt by being moved even seems to make our pain all the more acute.

As I look back, however, a most significant ingredient was the knowledge that every fracture meant not only certain kinds of physical indignities but also being wrenched away from home and family where, if there was confusion and perplexity, there was also love and security. This separation was extreme and very real because visiting was permitted only on Sundays for two hours and it was not always possible for my mother or grandparents to make that long trip every week. It was a long time before I fully appreciated the psychic scars caused by what inevitably I interpreted as "rejection."

Around these two realities—pain and separation— grew a constellation of others. Some of them almost seem contradictory. There was, for instance, a growing resentment about lack of privacy. For both practical and social reasons, I spent most of my childhood in the living room. The bed where I spent the first seventeen years of my life might literally have been at the center of the family's existence. In that sense, at least, I was anything but isolated. But it also meant that every function was performed in public, so to speak, subject to the scrutiny of others. And there have been times when I keenly felt that people somehow took for granted that they had a right to invade my privacy, indeed that I had no right to a private life. It was only a few years ago, when I was hospitalized for pneumonia, that an unfeeling doctor, without so much as a "with your permission," brought a colleague into my room, threw back the covers, and triumphantly pointed to my deformed legs. Oh, how I hated him!

Every person is entitled to a private sector in his life, where people are admitted only with his consent. It is in recognition of this that your mother and I have tried to respect your occasional insistence on closing us out of your room, and your right to play and phantasize without our always knowing what it represents.

Even though I was literally the center of the family's life, I felt a great sense of isolation as I grew older. Some families, embarrassed or even ashamed at having a crippled child in their midst, will in effect hide him away.

My isolation in fact as well as my feeling was not really the result of deliberate design by my family. I know that. Still some reality factors contributed to that isolation. One was that we lived on a farm, and the nearest neighbor was no closer than a quarter mile. Another was that there were no natural means of bringing me into contact with young people my age; most of my "friends" until college days were acquaintances of my mother or grandparents. And there was an understandable hesitancy on the part of the family to encourage such peer relationships even when they could because of the chronic anxiety that youthful exuberance might enhance the omnipresent dangers of physical harm. Furthermore, some parents have deepseated fears and prejudices about having their children associate with anyone who is "different." So there were not many my own age who ever found their way into our house.

    Even though you have gone to school and have had many more opportunities to relate to other children, I know you feel isolated sometimes. Sometimes you have been able to articulate your feelings, which has spurred your parents to struggle with new ways and means of bringing you into contact with other children. Both you and we have been grateful that there have been some neighbors or classmates whose parents have been willing to accept the risks and to permit you at least occasional access to their children's company. A few have even dared to invite you to spend the night in their homes. That kind of acceptance is still rare in our society, so its gracious quality is all the more apparent.

    As I grew older I became more conscious of my body. Gradually I came to loathe it. As a child I had been permitted—even encouraged—to walk a bit with heavy and hideous leg braces for support and a bit of protection. I still remember the little red wooden chair I pushed before me as I walked around the house or, occasionally, the hospital. There is a picture of me at age seven, sitting on the front steps, in which I am lean and straight and almost normal looking.

But then some stupid doctor decided, after I had fallen one day and broken my leg despite the protection of the braces, that I should not be permitted to walk again—it wasn't safe! And an equally ignorant physician somehow decided that perhaps I could be kept from breaking my legs if they were kept in plaster casts—as they were for many months. Add to the inactivity and inevitable atrophy such other inspired efforts as tinkering with my metabolism and "postponement" of corrections to deformities in my legs—and eventually you get the image with which I came to identify myself: someone soft, fat, and ugly.

Your mother says that I wrote her only one "love letter" during our courtship. Soon after she accepted my proposal of marriage, I made a trip. In a letter I expressed my great astonishment and joy that anyone as wonderful as she could bear to contemplate marriage with someone as grotesque as me. I revealed how I had put her to the test during the previous summer when we had gone to the beach and I had exposed my legs to her and had carefully recorded her immediate and her delayed reactions. You don't know how I dreaded that revelation. Yet, in a sense, you do because already you are concerned about the scars on your own legs and what people will say when they see them. Do you remember the discussion you had with your mother recently about leg makeup?

Unquestionably the intensity of my own feelings on this subject have made me ultrasensitive and militant over your appearance. That is why you are in the hospital now. Your last fracture turned out badly and you described the bow in your femur as "Mount Fuji" (since you were learning about Japan in social studies at the time)! We all knew that the suffering occasioned by correcting that now would be less than if we waited.

How we appear to ourselves—and how we think we appear to others—is more important than most people realize, this despite the fact that virtually everyone I know has some kind of "body image" problem, if only of incipient baldness or the appearance of lines in the face. Sometimes we decide to settle for the lesser of evils. I remember a very serious discussion with our beloved Dr. Wilson when I moved to New York. We carefully explored what would be involved in getting me out of my wheelchair and onto my feet. It would take a year at least, he told me, a year in which little could be dealt with except serial operations to correct deformities and periods of convalescence. Then would come an arduous period of learning to balance on my feet and the crutches which would become a part of me for the rest of my life. Aided by braces, he said, I should in time be able not only to stand but also to walk.

But I never decided to proceed with all this. Why? It was not because of the pain and effort involved. It was not even Phil's conclusion that I would still want to use my chair much of the time because of the physical demands that walking would entail. After all, people willingly undergo all kinds of inconvenience and suffering to achieve even a little more freedom of mobility. The decisive factor, I think, was the realization that unless I wanted to go a further radical step and have my legs amputated, I would be barely five feet tall and in some ways would be even more ridiculous a figure than I felt myself to be in my constant sitting position. Even though I fiercely resented being referred to as "a little man" (actually I am big framed and probably would have been at least six feet under normal circumstances), I concluded that I was a more impressive figure sitting down than I would be on crutches with people still towering over me.

Which means, of course, that even after my physical emancipation from confinement to bed and home I continued to be physically dependent for many needs. It is, as you already are beginning to understand, very galling to be unable to go everywhere you want and do whatever you want. Do you remember the day on the ferry in Bermuda last summer when you wanted your mother to carry you to the rail so that you could feel the spray from the rather choppy waves? She refused, and both of us were aware of some of the very practical reasons why. You are now big and heavy enough that carrying you is beginning to be a problem, and the footing on deck was not all that secure. But your face was, for an instant, a mask of tragedy; and I knew the disappointment and frustration you were experiencing.

I used to have a recurring phantasy when I was a kid (and it lasted well into adolescence), when even my strong grandfather could no longer lift and carry me. I dreamed of a superhuman man who would come into my life and be able to do all those things whenever I desired. It could only be a phantasy, and in due course there was adjustment to the fact that a wheelchair was much more practical.

I don't need to spell out for you how mobile I have become in a wheelchair. Yet there are physical barriers everywhere so that I need assistance—steep hills, rough terrain, most of all steps. I am both rather amused and appalled when I recall the countless times when, perhaps only for a brief time, rage has overcome me because of my dependency upon the help of others. More than once I have turned away from my objective rather than ask for help. By the same token, I have sometimes refused badly needed help because, for that moment, I could not face up to my need of it.

These are some of the things which create internal struggles and which leave scars . . . and from which I earnestly and impotently wished I could spare you as I have seen you experiencing them in your own life.

Still, in some sense, these are easier to deal with than some of the problems and frustrations other people impose on the physically handicapped. Anyone who is obviously different arouses a set of reactions which range from the annoying to the demeaning.

We are, for instance, chronic objects of curiosity. Do you remember that day in Rehoboth Beach, Delaware, when you turned your fury against a little boy? You were three or four at that time. Mummy had stopped in a store to buy something and you and I were waiting outside. A boy not much older than you spotted us, drew near, and subjected you to prolonged and unremitting staring. You stood it as long as you could, then visibly drew yourself up, and with great hostility in your voice demanded to know, "What you looking at, boy?" He fled in terror, even as I think I would have!

To have people stare at you like that is to make you wonder, "Am I some kind of freak?" I get particularly exercised when passers-by stop in their tracks and watch me attempt to negotiate a high curb or some other physical obstacle. Generally it makes me determined to "put on a good show" for them, to ask only for their disbelieving awe rather than their help; and having performed well, I am frequently tempted to lash out at them and say that I feel that I should expect them to pay "the price of admission" for the show.

Sometimes this curiosity gets the better of people and they want to get further satisfaction. So all kinds of impertinent questions are asked (one guy once even asked me how much money I had in the bank!), and most are miffed if you indicate even mildly that you consider these questions invasions of your private life.

There are, in human history, two common responses of the "normal" to the "abnormal." One is revulsion. To be in the presence of someone less than whole arouses in some individuals strong feelings—fear, disgust, perhaps even guilt. Even you have already had the experience of having terrified mothers pull their curious children away from any form of contact with you, as though you had some loathsome disease that might infect them. Many people consider any kind of physical impairment a curse; this "divine" disapproval might just "rub off" on them on too close association!

(This is why, I am convinced, it is common for panicked headwaiters to "hide" us as much as possible in restaurants. The number of times I have been relegated to the darkest and remotest recesses—usually near the kitchen door!—is legion, even though sometimes the desire to make me inconspicuous may result in great commotion, as other guests are required to make way for an inglorious procession that weaves among the tables to the ultimate hiding place.)

On the other hand, many people see us as something special, even bearers of "luck." God has a warm spot in his heart not only for fools and drunks, but also the handicapped! One day, when I was leaving a hospital after visiting a parishioner, a total stranger who had helped me down the front steps suddenly turned back to me and asked me for "three numbers." "You will bring me luck today," he said. Amused, I gave him the church's street address!

And there are some who still cling to the ancient belief that body contact with a cripple will bring good fortune, so they use all kinds of stratagems to touch or— better—rub your body. And still fairly numerous are those who believe that almsgiving is not only virtuous but also necessary to ward off evil. It distresses some to have me refuse money as they offer it on the street, and in other instances it confuses them because there is still a widespread conviction that all we are good for is begging.

Back about 1948 I spent Easter in Washington, D.C. I was feeling very well dressed in my new suit and my carnation boutonniere, and felt no embarrassment rubbing elbows with the fashionable congregation of the First Baptist Church (including President Truman). On my way back to the hotel, I asked a burly Naval officer for "a hand" up the curb. His response mystified me at first: "Gee, mister, it's been a long time since pay day." Then the light dawned. He had heard only what he expected to hear: "Give me a hand," i.e., some money. We finally sorted that one out and he helped me up onto the sidewalk.

But all these are slight annoyances compared to a couple of other assumptions about the physically handicapped. One is that no matter what their deficiency may be, they are also mentally incompetent. I was once exasperated enough to cry out to a personnel director in a job interview that I was not "selling" my legs but my brain, and that my brain did not happen to be located in my feet. It is almost hilarious how often it is assumed that I am a blithering idiot, totally incapable of understanding even the time of day. If someone is with me, this response is very common. I will ask a question; the answer is directed to my companion. In a restaurant one day I asked for a table for four and we were suitably directed to one. When we reached the table the same *maître d'* asked Mummy if "he will sit in his own chair?" On another occasion we purchased tickets for a movie, only to discover that there were no accessible seats. I asked for my money back and the manager instructed the cashier to prepare the necessary voucher. Then he presented the form to Mummy and asked her to sign. My wife—bless her—replied that he should give it to me, that not only could I speak, I could even sign my own name!

I still remember with some glee the time Preston Wilcox and I had lunch at a very fashionable restaurant where they obviously were unaccustomed to dealing with such customers as Blacks and cripples. I rather enjoyed the obvious indecision of the headwaiter—should he deal with Preston or with me? Finally Preston won out—whole Black men might just have a shade more intelligence than defective whites!

Which leads me to the other point: I really resent being treated as though I do not exist. When I applied at Union Seminary for the Master's program in religion and psychiatry, one of the things Charlie Stinnette asked me to do was to draw a picture of myself *and* another person. As I recall it, it was a street scene, with me talking to someone who was standing erect. Dr. Stinnette pointed out to me that the other person was not looking at me, but over my head. "That's the way you feel, isn't it? You see other people, but you don't feel they see you." And that was and is the case. You are not a person, but—if seen at all—a thing.

I guess I feel that way particularly when, as frequently happens, even with people whom I think should know better, someone comes up behind me on the street and starts pushing without any warning or any kind of inquiry as to whether that is what you desire. It's very unnerving to find yourself lurching forward; it's degrading to be considered something people can literally "push around" without question. It makes me angry, yet I know that one must be careful in his response to such treatment. Perhaps the most common myth people hold about the handicapped is that they are perpetually sweet, cheerful, patient, and long-suffering. Any deviation from this pattern wreaks consternation and great resentment.

You might get away with it, for crippled children arouse great emotional responses in people. They are cute oftentimes and their vulnerability elicits a desire to care for them and protect them against harm. Almost any kind of behavior by a child prompts an "isn't he cute?" kind of response. Because of your size and appearance, you still get this kind of response from most people, even though you are anything but childish in manner.

But when you become an adult, people find it harder to deal with your behavior patterns. No longer are you cute and defenseless. Indeed you may have developed some defenses which others find objectionable. You may drink or be abusive or whining or manipulative—anything but sweet, cheerful, patient, and long-suffering. And then it is that you really experience rejection. Society generally wants anyone who is visibly different to conform to its image of what he ought to be. To refuse is to risk denial of one's existence, to be treated as an invisible man. But to conform is also to deny one's true self; and looking back, I guess I would have to say that my adult life really has been one long act of defiance as I have tried to come to terms with myself and then to express that self honestly to all men. And that, Polly, has frequently been a lonely and painful struggle.

So this is the heritage I have bequeathed to you, and I guess at this point in my history I still have to say that I wish to God you could have been spared it.

It was the greatest day in my life when your mother agreed to marry me. Has she ever told you the story? One evening I took her to the Palace to see her favorite performer, Judy Garland. Afterward we went someplace to talk and she told me in detail why she had decided not to come to East Harlem as Bill Webber's secretary (which she had been at Union Seminary). As she talked on I almost lost the nerve I had built up through the preceding weeks to "pop the question" (silly expression, isn't it?). Somehow I clung to my resolve and finally, when there was a break in her narrative, I said, "I'd like to confuse the picture even more—would you marry me?" For virtually the only time in her life, your mother was speechless!

The course of true love, I have always been told, never runs smooth; and such was the course of mine. After some weeks of consideration, your mother agreed to marry me; but soon the pressures which had been building up caused her to write me a note saying it was all off and she was going to Boston to pull herself together. I was crushed, resentful, overwhelmed with the feeling that I had exceeded the bounds of what was right and proper. After all, what right did a cripple have to live what society calls "a normal life"? Helen Archibald, my advisor in the Group Ministry of the East Harlem Protestant Parish, tried to console me by telling me I should rely on my faith. I remember telling her somewhat petulantly that my faith had nothing to do with romance. Oh, how I hurt!

Then a call came from your mother. She had exercised her prerogative afresh and had changed her mind. She would marry me after all, if I would have her. I met her at the 125th Street Station with a box of candy on a cold winter's night, and our commitment to each other was reaffirmed in my tiny 100th Street apartment.

We were married in May, 1957. It was a very gay event. The wedding took place at the chapel of Union Seminary in the presence of an unbelievable number of well-wishing friends. The wedding night was in a suite at the Waldorf-Astoria (their generous interpretation of my request for a double room), the honeymoon in a second-rate hotel in Miami Beach.

Before the wedding I had been checked into the New York Hospital and was minutely gone over by internists, cardiologists, genito-urinary and orthopedic specialists. Bill Webber gave us our "marriage counseling" curiously—or appropriately—enough in my hospital room. The doctors I had asked assured me that in the absence of earlier familial history of *osteogenesis imperfecta* the odds were substantially in favor of our having normal and healthy children. So almost at once your mother and I deliberately tried to become parents. It was greatly frustrating to us both that it was nearly two years before your mother became pregnant.

You were upside down (in "breech," as the doctors less romantically call it) and no effort of the obstetrician could persuade you to turn around. So it was decided, in light of the fact that your mother was rather old to be having her first child, to play it safe and to deliver you by Caesarean section. I felt rather foolish and yet inordinately proud as I told people at a Protestant Council dinner, "Tomorrow I'm going to be a father!"

You were a beautiful baby, with great quantities of dark brown hair. I looked at you through the glass in utter disbelief that I could have had a part in producing anything so lovely and so perfect.

Then, three days later, Dr. Pierson called. He was a wonderfully urbane old man, with the "bedside manner" that has unhappily gone out of style with physicians. "I regret to tell you," he said, "Polly has a broken leg." There were some other details which hardly registered on my screaming brain. I thanked him politely, hung up the telephone, and then dissolved into the wracking dry sobs that only men can produce. Finally I was conscious of banging on the door. Two of our neighbors, who up to that time had hardly even acknowledged our existence on the floor, were shouting to me to unlock the door. Tears were streaming down my face as I did. "It's your daughter, isn't it?" one of them asked. I nodded. "Is there anything we can do?" I thanked them for their concern and said I thought I just needed some time alone to pull myself together.

You can't yet imagine how I felt, Polly—how guilty I felt, because I knew I was the one basically responsible for the fact that you would never be free from pain and limitation. Subsequent psychoanalysis helped me understand what I did that day. I compulsively called people to tell them the "news," apparently hoping that someone would vindicate my misery by berating me for what I had done. But no one did. Instead I learned what wonderful friends we had, as they sought to share the agony of that day. One who had not quite been sure that your mother should enter into this marriage sent me a compassionate note and a "little check"—$1,000—to help accomplish whatever was needed.

    I dreaded seeing your mother. But all she did was to embrace me and mingle her tears with mine. "We'll make it all right, baby," she said. "We gambled and lost," I said, and quickly she responded, "No, we won—we have a beautiful daughter."

    You were three days old when your beloved Dr. Wilson first saw you. "I'm sorry," he told me simply, putting his hand on my shoulder. "But I want you to know that Polly's condition is less severe than yours; and I want to tell you that we're going to know the solution to Polly's problem before she reaches adulthood." You know even better than I the meticulous, kind treatment that great orthopedic surgeon has given you through the years. I remember how another doctor expressed alarm to your mother, when you were about three, about the need for fairly drastic treatment of alleged muscle problems. But when you saw Dr. Wilson and he called you "sweetie" and gently felt your legs, you responded at once and exhibited great freedom in the use of all muscles. How fortunate you are to have that kind of doctor.

    Your mother developed an infection and so it was three weeks or more after your birth before you two could come home and I could hold you in my arms. How tiny, how fragile you seemed. It is said that there was something special between you and me from the start. Somehow I could quiet you when no one else could. Slowly I grew accustomed to the knowledge that I was a father, the father of a crippled child. I even managed to face with some equanimity your first fractures and your first marathon stays in the hospital. It was not until you got your first wheelchair (which made you very proud because you were now "just like daddy") that all the old emotions welled up again. Now the whole world would know what I had done to you!

After your birth all those purveyors of genetic optimism ran for cover. Your mother and I went to Johns Hopkins to see the leading authority in the genetics of *osteogenesis imperfecta*. He gently told us that the odds of having other defective children were no better than 50-50. So the decision to have no more children seemed inevitable. My best man, your godfather, Bill Stringfellow, went with me to see the doctor and to discuss the arrangements. I thought I was prepared to take the necessary steps until the night before my hospitalization when, suddenly, I panicked. I had to unburden myself to someone, so I stopped at Elmendorf Church. Don De Young sat on the steps to the sanctuary as I poured out my feelings about never being able to father another child. How kind he was, how understanding, how patient! He prayed in that rather incoherent fashion ministers necessarily adopt when they face real human crises. The important thing was that he stood by me in my hour of need. The operation took place and the only thing which alarmed the hospital personnel was that—as I always do when life becomes too much—I slept for almost twenty-four hours afterward, being only occasionally aware of a nurse asking if I were "all right."

And so, Polly, with varying degrees of composure and acceptance, I have seen you grow and suffer, and experience great joys as well. Believe me, there are no regrets about having you as my daughter. Quite the contrary. I take great pride in your development and accomplishments, and I love you with an intensity that sometimes frightens me. Since I can't spare you the pain and suffering, my hope is that somehow I can help you discover how to deal with them positively and as creatively as possible. That is why I vowed from the outset that some of my childhood experiences would not be repeated with you unless over my dead body. I have coveted for you the chance to achieve as much wholeness as is possible and to find as much joy and satisfaction as you can.

And that is a great deal. As I look back over what I have written, I am a bit fearful that I may have persuaded you that life is grim and burdensome. You know that is not the way I feel. In many ways I consider myself to be among the most privileged of men, for my life has been exciting and—I hope—worthwhile.

That is why I have decided to write you these letters. You will understand them better in a few years. But even now I hope I can share some things with you that will at least preserve your hope that the end of the struggle is not despair but hope and joy.

Good night, Pussy Cat.

Daddy

Liberation

2

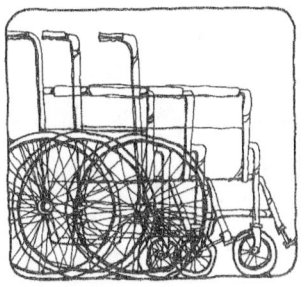

Dear Polly

A popular word these days among people all over the world who are trying to change the circumstances of their lives is "liberation." That, I think, is a good word for me to use about my own life; for I think you will agree that I have achieved a considerable degree of freedom from the frustrations and limitations of being physically handicapped. It has been a long time since anyone referred to me—as they occasionally do to you—as "you poor thing!" I clearly am not a "thing"—a stubborn, dogmatic, volatile personality perhaps, but hardly a "thing." And I am anything but poor—except perhaps in money. I am not "putting you on" when I say that I consider myself a very fortunate, even privileged, person. I am rich in experiences and friendships, in memories and expectations. So this letter and those which will follow will attempt to describe some of the significant factors in my "liberation."

It began with the church, Polly. That may surprise you, since you are going through a very antireligious period these days. (That seems to be a rather common experience for any "p.k.") It surprises many people, as a matter of fact, for this is an age when few expect anything good to come out of the church. Still I guess I have to say that one should *expect* the church to be the arena where one begins to know and to use his freedom.

My family was pretty active in the church, especially my grandparents. The local pastor would come to call occasionally; and I looked forward to these visits, since he generally was a student, young, intelligent, bringing a welcome bit of the "world" into our circumscribed farm household. My grandfather's brother, Caspar Garrigues, was also a clergyman; and I eagerly anticipated the all too infrequent visits of that kindly, urbane, and generous spirit. Even though there was a difference of fifty or more years in our ages, he had a wonderful facility of making me feel his equal, and of stimulating my mind to wrestle with ideas which rarely were otherwise discussed in our household. He died a few years ago, nearly a hundred years old, alert, interested, and interesting to the last. I often thought that if I could grow old so gracefully as he had done, old age would indeed be nothing to fear or regret.

After my mother remarried and we left my grandparents' home, even this tenuous tie to the church was broken for a time. Then one day the aggressive young Presbyterian minister stopped at our house to ask directions to a neighbor's. My mother invited him in, and in the course of an intense hour's conversation he persuaded me that I should "confess my sins and accept the Lord Jesus Christ as Savior." It was an emotion-packed experience. I really did feel sinful at that point, much more about adolescent phantasies than overt behavior; and it did not take undue pressure to get me to reach out for forgiveness and help.

The next day I wrote Uncle Cap (as all of us called him) and told him about my "decision for Christ." I was disappointed, I added, because I found that I actually felt no different that morning than I had the day before. The same dreams, the same thoughts, the same pressures were there. His reply was irenic and reassuring. While he did not use such language, what he tried to convey to me was the reality that the Christian life is one of "becoming"—a progressive, developing, deepening kind of experience. The key to it all, he said, was to remember that the God revealed in Jesus Christ loves us no matter how we feel at any given moment, is not "put off" by our failures, and is ever standing by to lend his strength to us as we take the next step forward.

Looking back on this, I can identify it as a providential event. And equally providential was the sudden appearance of Charles McCarty, then pastor of the First Baptist Church in Monon, Indiana. He had heard of me, he said, and had wanted for some time to get acquainted with me. In the ensuing months we became very close friends and confidants. Charles was generally considered to be a bit "liberal," not so much because his theology was suspect but because his interests were wide ranging and he had the reputation of speaking his mind about many issues. Furthermore, his wife was vivacious, liked to wear bright colors, and did her ironing late at night. Certainly that was enough to ruin any small-town minister's reputation!

From the beginning we shared confidences, mutually stretched our minds discussing, sometimes arguing, about ideas which most residents of Monon would have found incomprehensible if not seditious. During his frequent visits Charles encouraged me to air my questions about the Christian faith. Still a student himself, he shared his books with me, as well as his reactions to what his professors told him in class. He was the first person to demonstrate to me that one could not have all the answers but still maintain a vital belief in God.

Then Easter Sunday drew near, and Charles asked if I would be interested in attending the worship service at the church. He persuaded my mother that sufficient manpower would be provided to protect me from any physical danger. I came home ecstatic, not only stirred by the music and the symbolic acts of the occasion, but deeply moved by the genuinely cordial reception of the congregation. My coming had obviously been no surprise; Charles had prepared them well.

I later learned that it was a layman in that small-town congregation who raised the question why such visits to the church could not be made a regular thing. And in quick order a half-dozen or so men volunteered to take turns in picking me up on Sundays. Indeed I soon became one of the most faithful attenders at Sunday services!

Then I was asked if I would be willing to prepare the church bulletin for mimeographing. Invitations began to come to take part in other church activities, to join the newly formed young-adult group, for example. And eventually I was asked to serve on church committees, to read the Scripture at the Christmas-eve service, to substitute as a Sunday school teacher.

Somewhere along the way Charles had asked me if I would like to be baptized and join the church. I enthusiastically agreed; and on a Sunday night, in the strong but gentle hands of the pastor and a burly deacon, I was plunged beneath the waters of the church's tiny baptistry. That is how I became a Baptist. I think it is fair to acknowledge that had the historical circumstances been different and Charles McCarty had been an Episcopalian or the local congregation had been Methodist, I would just as happily have affiliated with another branch of Christ's Church. For what I joyously joined that day was a congregation of the faithful—fearfully weak and sometimes tragically divided, yet understanding and believing enough to care and to welcome. It was, with all its warts, truly the body of Christ in that place.

Charles McCarty exercised a tremendous influence over my life, providing me with models for manhood and humanity which still are meaningful. None was greater than what might be called "the suffering servant."

The doctors had never really been honest with me through my childhood and adolescence. While progressively postponing the date of deliverance, consistently they dangled before me the hope—no, almost the promise—that at some point I would become "normal" and would be freed of physical shackles. It all seems rather silly now—how, in the face of all too obvious reality, I permitted myself to indulge in such dreams. Perhaps I still thought of doctors as miracle workers, not unlike Mandrake the Magician who was one of my favorite comic-strip characters in those days.

By the time I was about twenty, and had begun to taste the excitement of even tentative forays into the wider world, I insisted during a clinic visit that I wanted a realistic appraisal of what I could expect to be and do in the future. Could I, specifically, leave home, go to college, begin to live a more active life? So I was x-rayed from head to foot; every muscle and nerve was prodded and tested. I was promised a full report in a few weeks.

I guess I knew when I returned to the clinic that some illusions of the past would have to die. A nervous, embarrassed, inexperienced young intern was commissioned to break the news. It was the experts' considered judgment that I would never walk. I absorbed that reasonably well. If, I asked, I must think in terms of using a wheelchair for the rest of my life, how active could I be? The recommendation essentially was that I should stay at home and exercise caution, that otherwise the risk of further and perhaps more serious fractures was great. In stunned disbelief, I asked, "Are you telling me I can't go to college?" "Absolutely not," was the reply, "it is too dangerous."

Many times during my childhood I had heard medical personnel express surprise that I had survived in relatively good shape, since in that primitive time prior to the antibiotics and sulfa drugs most victims of *osteogenesis imperfecta* succumbed to secondary infections associated with multiple broken bones. On that night, for the first time in my life, I regretted that I had not died.

The next evening Charles came to see me. I was

obviously depressed and needed to tell him only a little to give him a clear picture of how disappointed I was. I don't remember what he said; the words were not all that numerous or important. What counted was that he, too, was disappointed and that he stayed with me for a long time that night. It was a magnificent demonstration of solidarity of one human being with another.

As he left he invited me to go on a picnic with his family the next day. I went, and as I reached for something during the meal—in an incredible demonstration of clumsiness—I managed to turn my chair over and to find myself sprawling on the ground. Time stood still for me and for the anxious McCartys bending over me. I shook myself, then announced triumphantly, "Nothing's broken!" Charles told me later, "I knew then you had won a great victory."

And so I had. I did go on to college, but more about that later. And wondrously in Crawfordsville there was another concerned and congenial congregation, and another supportive minister, George King. A few people doubtless had questions about my orthodoxy even then, but the Christians at First Baptist stood by me loyally through crisis and accomplishment. They even suffered through my very first sermon—all forty-five minutes of it —and were gracious enough to encourage me to try again!

It was there, near the end of my junior year, that one Sunday morning I was overwhelmed with the feeling that God wanted me to give my life to what middle-western Protestants call "full-time Christian service." I found myself responding to the invitation at the end of the service and informing the congregation of my decision. Subsequently, I had some doubts about it, particularly about my motivations—perhaps I was doing this only out of a sense of gratitude for what the church had meant to me during the few years before. I remember talking about this with Harry Cotton, the perceptive and wise professor of philosophy at my college. He told me that the burden of deciding whether this vocational choice was right was not mine alone, that historically the church has had a peculiar ability to tell whether any man has been called by God. And in that congregation there appeared to be no doubts.

So then the question became how to acquire the necessary preparation, indeed to decide what form that ministry would take. There were some sentimental souls in the Crawfordsville church who felt that I would make a sensational evangelist. Because of a persistent interest in psychology, I rather inclined toward some kind of counseling ministry. But the decision was not pressing. Partly because I was tired of studying and wanted to earn some money, and partly because none of the top-rank theological schools was willing to accept me as a student (except Union, which said it would think about it), I went to Indianapolis and threw myself zestfully into a job as a medical secretary at Indiana University Medical Center where for many years I had been a frequent patient.

Once again I was fortunate to find some extraordinary Christians. First Baptist was a large congregation, considerably wealthier and more sophisticated than I had experienced before. There were numbers of intelligent and attractive young people, and my social life flourished as I dated the most intelligent and attractive of the eligible girls! Eventually I was ordained in that church.

And in Indianapolis, too, I found another person who took great interest in my intellectual and spiritual development. Gertrude Gunn was my boss at the Medical Center, an Episcopalian who has never really given up hope that I might someday join "the true church"! At her insistence I went to talk to the people at Butler School of Religion (now Christian Theological Seminary) about the possibility of enrolling part-time. When that seemed feasible, Gert allowed me to juggle my working hours to make it possible.

For my first vacation I came to New York on a Greyhound bus. It was my second visit to the city we all call "home." The first had ended disastrously a few years before when a taxi accident on 42nd Street sent me to the Hospital for Special Surgery for four months with multiple fractures. In part, I guess, I wanted to overcome the "jinx"! The chief reason for the trip, however, was to visit Union Seminary and to persuade the officials if I could that I was sufficiently intelligent and mobile to make the grade. Apparently I succeeded; for despite some nervous second thoughts as the time for my arrival as a student approached, I was made very welcome.

I spent two marvelous years at Union. Because of the inaccessibility of the dining room, I was housed on a married-students' floor in the dormitory. I had learned to be a good cook during college days and had perfected my culinary skills while maintaining a bachelor apartment in Indianapolis. At Union I was soon happily trading recipes and menus with the student wives in the community kitchen. One of them told me years later how, initially, they had all conspired to "take care" of me by inviting me for meals. But soon they discovered that the invitations were being returned and that I usually fed them more sumptuously than they did me! So things began to settle down to a more normal kind of relationship.

One of the more hilarious incidents at Union was the insistence of the housekeeper that I have access to the ladies' room, since it had the only bathtub on the floor. An elaborate system was devised—but seldom used—to determine whether "the coast was clear" and signs prepared for posting to warn the girls when I had invaded their quarters.

Playing bridge was one of my favorite pastimes, and I found any number of like-minded people around. The best theology encountered in those two years came not from books but in discussions late at night as we drank coffee and took time out from serious card playing.

Needless to say, I became perhaps the best known person around the seminary. In my senior year Bill Webber, then the dean of students, asked me to become one of his assistants and just to continue what I already was doing—trying to be responsive to the various kinds of crises which even theological students knew in abundance.

Another rewarding thing to come out of the Union experience was my introduction to Harlem. Every student was required to take "field work" in order to get some practical experience in some kind of church setting. The Seminary felt the ideal solution was to place me as a Sunday school teacher at Riverside Church, which is just across the street. The minister of education there had other ideas, though; he turned me down because I had not had, in his words, "a normal adolescence"—whatever that may be!

So with some embarrassment and hesitancy, the director of field work asked if I would mind working in a "Negro church." I said nothing would please me more. The next year was spent at the Church of the Master, where I learned that Christian graces know no racial barriers; there I found another compassionate congregation and another great pastor, Jim Robinson. It was he who later preached my ordination sermon and then at my installation at Chambers Church.

My specific task was to teach a small twelfth-year Sunday school class and to act more or less as a doorman at a weekday junior high recreation program. Without anyone's realizing it, that year at Church of the Master was to set the stage for my future ministry. (Parenthetically I should tell you that the next year, with a change of personnel, I was invited to join the teaching staff at Riverside!)

But the most momentous event of my Union Seminary experience was to meet your mother. She had begun her job as dean's secretary just a few days before I arrived. I went into Bill Webber's office and announced to the attractive lady there, "I'm Mel Schoonover." "Yes, I know!" was the spirited response. She likes to tell people how the dean's staff wrestled with the problem of what they were "going to do with this guy in a wheelchair," and how she took care of the matter once and for all—"I married him!"

Then graduation came. We all were a bit concerned, I suppose, about what was to happen to me. Bob Handy— the only Baptist on the Union faculty—had gotten all the Baptist executives together to meet me and to think about some kind of placement. The best they could do was to invent a job for me in the Board of Education and Publication; but no matter how I tried to conjure up another definition, it was clear I was to be a well-paid file clerk and I declined the offer as graciously as possible.

A second job offer was from First Baptist in Indianapolis to return as their minister of education. Even then I had great doubts about the value of most of what masquerades as Christian education; and furthermore I already was a controversial figure in that congregation because of my stand on race, so I decided that I would decline the offer rather than risk being fired in a few months.

That left me with the invitation I accepted. Bill Webber had decided to leave Union Seminary to work full time for East Harlem Protestant Parish, which he had helped to found a few years before. He asked me to come along and to take on the task of administering a program that had proliferated in all directions. At that point I was incredibly ill informed about the problems of inner-city ministry. I knew next to nothing about East Harlem. Perhaps if I had known more about either, I might have decided I had neither preparation nor skill to offer in a setting like that. But ignorance was a form of bliss, and I launched into the job with characteristic enthusiasm. I confess that I almost threw in the towel after the first summer. My first responsibility was to see that two hundred children got off to "friendly town" vacations in the country. Mainly it was the frequent necessity of getting up at 5:00 a.m. to be sure that stragglers were rounded up and everyone delivered to the train on time that almost stripped me of all my religion and commitment to the ministry!

Otherwise I loved East Harlem, with all its dirt and disorganization and decay. And, as you well know, that love affair persists even now. It seems almost inconceivable that we should live anywhere else. The chief joy of the early years was not in manipulating the powers of the administrator in keeping wheels turning but in coming to know people of incredibly diverse backgrounds who were more or less successful in surviving the cruelty and deprivations and injustices of a society which labeled them "undesirable." Somehow I felt very much at home with the people of East Harlem; I felt no fear wandering the streets at any hour. My tiny ground-floor apartment on 100th Street was robbed once, but even the junkies took a protective attitude toward my person.

After a time, however, I began to be fed up with shuffling papers and keeping the administrative machinery functioning smoothly. I wanted to be out in the streets more, to spend more time with the people than with the gifted but frequently exasperating staff. An inquiry from a midwestern college about my possible availability for a chaplaincy position gave me a pretext to raise the question of redefinition of role. The upshot of it all was that the college job never materialized (concern was expressed about my physical mobility) and I was disillusioned to discover that the Group Ministry of the Parish had no more confidence in my ability to function as a pastor than the people in the college town. The congregation of one of the store-front churches was willing to have me as their minister, but the staff (which firmly controlled the Parish at that point) selected someone else. It was not without a considerable degree of feeling of bitterness and betrayal that I rejected the offer of some vague free-floating ministry and decided to leave.

Somewhat earlier I had informally discussed with R. LaRue Cober at the New York Baptist City Society the possibility of becoming minister of Chambers Memorial in the north end of East Harlem. I knew that Jim Bartlett (a frequent bridge partner from Union days) was about to leave his part-time pastorate there; and he had frequently expressed his hope that the mission society would attempt to revitalize that church by bringing in more experienced and full-time leadership. My inquiries of the Society produced discouraging responses; I felt that once again the fact that I was in a wheelchair was the decisive factor.

That meant that I left East Harlem Protestant Parish with no job at all. Your mother's Aunt Lucy had recently died, leaving a legacy large enough for an extensive trip to Europe. When we returned to New York three months later, there still was no job. Mummy got a secretarial job at Riverside Church, and I returned to Union Seminary to work on a master's degree.

We had hardly gotten settled in there when Jim Bartlett awakened us late one night by pounding on our apartment door. He was jubilant—the Chambers congregation had voted to extend me a call to be its pastor and the City Society had concurred. So back to East Harlem we went. And for the next ten years, as you well know, I was caught up in a ministry that was frequently frustrating, chronically exhausting, and always exciting. Few people have been so privileged as I was to be an active participant in a social revolution. Not only did I have the chance to be pastor and preacher in fairly traditional terms, but also the opportunity to become an unsuccessful politician, a moderately successful community organizer, and a very successful "trouble maker" in various aspects of community life.

The amazing thing about it was that at Chambers, too, I found imaginative, sensitive, and courageous Christians. They were intensely loyal to me and were willing to back me to the hilt whenever my "wheeling and dealing" brought criticism and attack. And by the same token, I was loyal to them and frequently found myself agreeing to do unfamiliar things because they pressed me to join with them in tackling all kinds of human needs. When I think back over those years and their fantastically varied involvements—work with gangs and addicts, welfare struggles, urban-renewal battles, the development of housing, a short-lived but intensely exciting foray into local politics, the encouragement of the school decentralization experiment at I.S. 201, involvement with East River CORE, and so on—I realize afresh how it could never have happened unless the church had really been present—a band of saintly sinners, manifesting to the world those perceptive words of St. Paul: *But we have this treasure in earthen vessels, to show that the transcendent power belongs to God and not to us. We are afflicted in every way, but not crushed; perplexed, but not driven to despair; persecuted, but not forsaken; struck down, but not destroyed; always carrying in the body the death of Jesus, so that the life of Jesus may also be manifested in our bodies* (II Corinthians 4:7-10—RSV).

When we knew of your physical problem, I asked Thelma Cockerham what people in the church were saying —did they think we were foolish for having taken the risk of having children? Her reply sort of characterized the attitude of the people at Chambers toward us and toward everyone: "No. They're saying you've had a tough break. Their only question is how can they help?"

Their generosity and willingness to share extended even to my services. They thought it quite appropriate that I give time to help train prospective ministers, so for ten years I counseled a succession of wonderful young men and women who came to spend a year or two at Chambers as field workers. The congregation also warmly supported my chaplaincy work at *our* hospital (Special Surgery) where, for six years, I had a chance to help hundreds of orthopedic patients work through some of the personal crises they were experiencing—and in the process meet such fascinating people as the Duchess of Windsor, Charles Laughton, and Cornelia Otis Skinner.

Common to all these experiences, I suppose, is a compassionate, supportive community. Oh, I know, every one of the congregations I have known has had more than its share of problems. The Indiana congregations spent far too much time and energy quarreling about secondary theological issues and far too little time dealing with primary social issues. As for Chambers, one member once made the assessment that there wasn't a single "sane" person in the entire congregation. Yet in every instance a genuine community of love and support existed despite everything, so that I—and others, too—found it possible to grow, to work out some of my "hang-ups," and at least to move toward that goal of freedom which I firmly believe was the function of Jesus' whole ministry and teaching.

To experience that is to experience grace, to know how much luckier you are than you deserve to be. It is to learn that the things which keep one alive, which make humanity human indeed, are gifts. Since real gifts have no strings attached, are never debts which must be repaid, one is free to respond as he is able; and that response, at its best, is to begin giving gifts—to pass the grace on, so to speak.

In such a community one can dare to believe that the nature of reality is basically benevolent—that God both loves and is love. It is to discover that that love encompasses every man, the whole world, the whole creation; and that one is free to give himself to all kinds of ridiculous "causes" in the attempt to make God's will "done on earth as it is in heaven." There is in the church, then, the freedom to make mistakes as well as to succeed, to engage in that painful but glorious process of growth which leads to greater freedom. All this because, as St. Paul so eloquently put it, *"Love is patient and kind; love is not jealous or boastful; it is not arrogant or rude. Love does not insist on its own way; it is not irritable or resentful; it does not rejoice at wrong, but rejoices in the right. Love bears all things, believes all things, hopes all things, endures all things"* (I Corinthians 13:4-7—RSV).

In the church that love can be seen, celebrated, and proclaimed. The church, when defined that way, is, it seems to me, something worth defending, something worth giving one's strength and skill and loyalty. That kind of church can help people reach liberation.

You asked Mummy a while back, "Is Daddy still a minister?" I can understand your confusion, for it has been nearly two years since I left Chambers. There are now only rare sermons to prepare, and we frequently find excuses to do other things on Sunday rather than going to church.

I felt I had to leave Chambers, Polly. It had become a great conviction that for me to cling to the position I held, when all the time I argued that black people should assume responsibility for their own affairs and control their own institutions, was somehow at least inconsistent and perhaps downright hypocritical. I guess I hoped that some other congregation would want me as their minister. Indeed I was rather eager to go to a different kind of church, even one in an affluent suburb, to see whether what I had learned about the potentialities of the church in East Harlem could be found elsewhere. Certainly I advertised my availability as widely as I could in that decorous fashion that is supposedly "proper" for clergymen. It hurt to learn little by little that I had at least four drawbacks, as far as those in position to aid placement were concerned:

    a) I was labeled as an "inner city expert"—which presumably meant that I was disqualified to serve anywhere else;

    b) I was a "controversial figure"—I dabbled in politics;

    c) I was "too expensive"—after all, Chambers (a mission church, would you believe?) paid me the shockingly high salary of $8,000 per year;

    d) and, apparently still very decisive, I was physically handicapped. So there were no offers from the church. In a sense perhaps one could say that I did not leave the church, but the church left me!

    And so, as you know, I am now a "consultant." I do many things for many people—teach, lecture, write, advise, plot and plan. But am I a minister? The answer is unqualifiedly "Yes!" If I have come to be sure of anything in my life it is in Providence. I do not have much clarity at this point about my future "job description." About my vocation there is no uncertainty: I am a Christian, and *all* Christians, regardless of what they do and where they work, are ministers. So I shall try to practice that vocation wherever I am, and faithfully participate in the ministry established by Christ when he stood in the synagogue in his home town and announced that his mission in life was to preach good news to the poor, to proclaim release to captives and recovering of sight to the blind, to set at liberty those who are oppressed, and to proclaim God's acceptance of us all.

Till next time, my beloved Polly,

Daddy

Travel

3

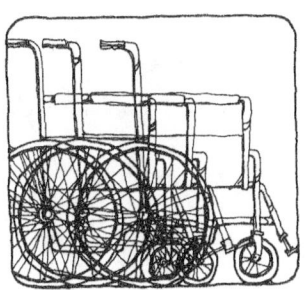

Dear Polly

When through the years people have commented on my "courage" in trying to lead a full and active existence, I have frequently responded that what they characterized as courage has often been no more than the judicious application of a shove from the rear. Everyone can look back and identify a few people who were especially influential in his life. I can think of a half-dozen or so. None, I suppose, did more to help me achieve liberation than Ken Miller.

He was on leave for military service during World War II from his position as executive of the Indiana Society for Crippled Children when I first came to know that organization. His staff had been well trained and they exhibited a compassionate and generous spirit in trying to figure out what could be done to make my life more satisfying and fulfilling. Over a period of time, they did several things, like providing me with my first folding wheelchair, paying the tuition for two or three correspondence courses (including one in shorthand, of all things!), and sponsoring for four years a little magazine for handicapped people which I had helped to found and which I edited with—hopefully—growing skill for most of that time.

So I had begun the process of emancipation even before I met Ken Miller. He was to provide a boost, however, that still has me moving outward. It happened like this:

I had gone to spend a few days with Florence Pettit and her children. She was another compassionate and concerned person who gave me, incidentally, the first encyclopedia I ever owned. She had persuaded my mother of her trustworthiness as a surrogate parent, and so I was permitted to have this brief time away from home. Florence asked if there was anything in particular I would like to do and, rather to my surprise, I found myself boldly saying I would like to go to Indianapolis (about 50 miles away) where the annual meeting of the Easter Seal Society was taking place. My surprise was increased when she readily agreed.

Ken Miller welcomed me warmly and made certain that I met as many people as possible. A subject of great interest at the meeting was the national convention soon to be held in Chicago. (This was 1946, the first year really that people were beginning to resume the observances and celebrations which had been suspended during the war years.) As the day came to a close, Ken stopped to talk with me. How would I like to go to the Chicago convention as the Indiana Society's guest? I said nothing would please me more, but I was sure my mother would never consent. So Ken appealed to my love of conspiracy and suggested that I wire the Palmer House for a reservation immediately and then tell her that all arrangements had been made and wouldn't it be too bad to disappoint everyone, etc.

All my life I had been surprised by unexpected turns of events, and my surprise was great when my mother said she thought it would be all right. So off to Chicago I went, alone, on the Monon Railroad. When I got to the hotel, Ken Miller told me I was to do whatever I wanted, that here was some money for incidental expenses and more could be provided as needed. For four or five days I deliriously sampled my new-found freedom. I took taxis all over the city. I wheeled along State Street and Michigan Boulevard window shopping, and I went night-clubbing with new friends. (I also learned a few lessons in social protocol as, for example, when a foreign-accented headwaiter refused me entrance to a hotel dining room until I returned properly clad in coat and tie!) And during those few days I learned that while I still needed a lot of help at steps and curbs and revolving doors, I really could be out in the world, on my own. When I thanked Ken for my glorious "learning experience," he responded with the assurance that he felt Easter Seal money had never been so wisely invested.

And, as you very well know, I have not stopped "traveling" since. That experience in Chicago only whetted my appetite to explore strange places. The appetite had been there all along. When our visits to Indianapolis were just for routine examinations, I eagerly looked forward to them—and usually managed to persuade my indulgent grandfather to drive around the Circle and out past the Governor's mansion. There had also been a quick trip to Chicago one Saturday in my childhood to attend the National Barn Dance. I thought and talked about that experience for years. And I greedily devoured the books of Richard Halliburton in which that strange man described his visits to exotic lands in a time when travel took more courage and resourcefulness. I considered it a personal loss when his raft was lost in a Pacific storm and he presumably drowned in quest of still another travel epic.

I phantasized a great deal about visiting such places myself. At one point I had a complete set of Shell Oil Company road maps and daydreamed about "hitchhiking" across our own country. Another early "hobby" was making lists of hotels all over the world; these, too, were incorporated in my game-playing. I acted out all kinds of adventures with the boy and girl dolls my family provided among my many toys. The psychological implications are pretty obvious now in those imagined climbings of great mountains, or trekkings across vast deserts, or explorations of romantic Eastern kingdoms. I guess I alternated between the roles of villain and hero. But phantasy, however rich, is a poor substitute for the real thing.

So I vowed that I would see as much of this world as I could. Before and during college days, there were a few trips to places like Washington and Philadelphia and Kansas City. There was even a trip to New York in the middle of my junior year which ended disastrously in a taxi accident on 42nd Street with multiple fractures of my left leg. Even a hospitalization of four months a thousand miles from home was not enough to curb my ardor for travel.

Then, after college, I began to explore other parts of the country by bus, getting to Miami Beach one year and parts of the Far West another. In more recent years the chance has come to visit other countries, to make the whole world the arena for exploration. And today I am more convinced than ever that travel has been—and I trust will continue to be—one of the most liberating factors in my life.

That is why we have introduced you to the excitement and joy of travel very early. There have been many who think we are nuts. We spend all of our surplus money—and then some!—on travel, instead of being prudent and saving our money for what may well be inevitable future physical crises. We run the risk of having broken bones in remote places where medical care may be of a less sophisticated order than we know in New York. Indeed, your travels have included visits to hospitals in Bermuda and Antigua. In the latter, even in pain, you were amused to see goats grazing in a courtyard as you were taken from the emergency room to the operating theater. Injuries notwithstanding, we still go because we know that for us there may be no tomorrow, no future possibility to savor the color and drama and fulfillment of dreams that seeing new places, doing new things, and meeting new people has brought.

Travel for us has not been completely without its problems, of course. It is, for one thing, expensive. Even though we rarely travel first class, it turns out to be even more costly since wheelchairs and other unusual items of luggage make it necessary to have more help and therefore to dispense more tips. And frequently we find we have to stay in first-class hotels or eat in expensive restaurants because these are more likely to have large elevators and wide doors.

But even doing this does not solve all the accessibility problems. It constantly angers me that architects and builders incorporate unnecessary physical barriers in tourist and other public facilities. I can understand why the catacombs in Rome can be reached only via long flights of stairs and narrow corridors, but I fail to comprehend why modern facilities have to duplicate these hurdles. And my biggest gripe of all, as you know, is about the "economies" effected by greedy businessmen when they authorize twenty-two-inch doors for what may otherwise be an enormously roomy bathroom. It does not mean that I wet my pants, but it does mean that relieving myself becomes a constant exercise in gymnastics and ingenuity.

When we were in Antigua, we met an architect from Buffalo who had just recently been appointed to an "architectural barriers committee." "I never realized," he told me, "how we make your life miserable by our insensitivity to your needs—how two steps are as much of a problem oftentimes as six, how doors are too narrow or swing the wrong way, how ordinary things like water fountains and urinals are hung too high, and so on." Not all architects are so easily converted. I remember another who dismissed most of my "gripes" on the ground that people like me were only occasional users of public buildings, although he had no ready answer to my retort that more of us might use them if people like him did not always throw barriers in the way.

But some people are sensitive and considerate. The conversation with the Buffalo architect took place at the Callaloo Beach Hotel where Edie and Tommy Keasbey even laid down plywood walks so that we would have as few problems as possible. And I think we are at least partially responsible for their decision to build the showers so that people in wheelchairs could "drive in" if they want. And you remember Barb and Cyril Cooper at "Rosemont" in Bermuda who not only put unnecessary ramps here and there and asked me to check their plans for new units so that the doors would be wide enough and the toilets accessible (although the Bermuda Planning Authority vetoed their plan to install grab bars as a "hazard"), but boldly advertise in their new brochure that they "welcome" handicapped guests. This is not the only reason why the Keasbeys and the Coopers are among our favorite friends!

In fact, it is not just the insensitive architects and the stupid planners. The chief problem every handicapped traveler confronts is rigid human attitudes. A lot of people in the tourist industry are inexperienced in dealing with the handicapped and have no particular desire to change the fact. A few are downright hostile; you get the impression that they hope that you will be frightened off and leave them alone. I am often tempted to tell them that we are going to be increasingly in evidence and they may as well adjust to that reality.

But more often the problem is with personnel who take refuge behind "standard operating procedures" even if they are clearly inappropriate. Airline personnel are the worst. Sometimes they get downright hysterical when confronted with wheelchairs. The sight of two of them at one time seems to bring virtual panic. You remember how more than once on our trip to Africa we were asked to "keep calm," although we were not the people who were excited! My hunch is that airline people get less upset if they have not been warned of our arrival in advance. They have less time in which to generate anxieties.

Of course most airlines get very exercised if they are not informed ahead of time so that "proper arrangements" can be made. Those arrangements sometimes verge on indignity. I have spent much time in airports waiting for them to be completed, with my pleas to be permitted to get myself on or off the plane persistently ignored. After all, with their accumulated experience, what could I possibly know. The inference is that I am a handicapped person and everyone knows that, as such, my mental competency is always subject to question.

Sometimes I fight the system; sometimes I acquiesce. If it is a new airline, I am generally curious as to what new wrinkle will be exposed. They all seem to be different. Some of the major European airlines virtually ignore you, seemingly considering their responsibility to be limited to selling you a ticket. You have to remind them that your chair is to go on the plane with you. Other lines want handicapped persons to be carried on board by their own personnel, others by ambulance attendants. Some airlines use forklifts to get us on board. You remember the fun we had in Tel Aviv when all three Schoonovers were put on a forklift at the terminal and driven across the tarmac to the waiting plane.

But that, of course, was nothing compared to the treatment we received in London where we were met by *two* ambulances and a "matron." At some of the African airports I visited before you and Mummy joined me, the local manager would personally come to superintend the loading or unloading. Once, when it was raining, I rode in his Mercedes limousine!

And sometimes we are victims of "mistakes," as when seat assignments are made near doors that are not being used for boarding. By the same token, however, we have just as often been the recipients of undeserved "favors," as when we have been put in first-class accommodations because some airline authority felt that these would be more comfortable or convenient. And several times abroad, on long layovers between connecting planes, airlines have wanted to put us in hotels so that we could rest. I know that some of this is concern about minimizing problems and possible complaints or lawsuits; nonetheless, we have met countless people accommodating and helpful far in excess of the need.

Despite them, there are still many things we simply have to do for ourselves if travel is to be possible. I long ago decided, Polly, that I had a choice of staying home or of resorting to undignified postures in order to cover as much ground as possible. For that reason I seek out alleys and back doors if these are easier to negotiate than the "public" entries. I have gone through countless kitchens and garages and pump rooms and garbage areas in order to be as independent of help as possible. I almost spit in the eye of the officious travel agent in Israel who had booked us constantly into hotels with many steps (he had not bothered to read all the requirements listed by our New York agent) and then took umbrage because I demanded to explore the service entrances.

And equally I have learned how to sit on the arms of my chair in order to narrow it enough to fit through small openings. I have been willing to get out of my chair and scoot up or down a flight of stairs on my fanny in order to get places otherwise inaccessible. (That's how I saw some of the catacombs!) I have clambered over tree trunks and slid down hills. And hundreds of times I have entrusted my safety to people whose experience in handling wheelchairs seemed closely parallel to their lack of knowledge of English. Foolish? Probably. Yet the end result is that I have been able to get far more places than many people with two good legs.

Yet travel for people like us inevitably has an element

of frustration. There are some places one simply cannot get to, places which must be explored from afar or only in one's imagination. Most beaches are like that, since we do not track very well in sand. The Moslem mosque in Nairobi was such a place, too, for a different and quite humorous reason: I was refused admission because of my equivalent of shoes— the tires on my chair! The Parthenon in Athens is another example. But do you remember how we sat on an adjoining hill and were entranced for an hour as our lovely young guide painted word pictures of what we would see if we climbed the steep and broken steps and looked first this direction, then that? It was an exciting experience for us all, and a triumphant one for her as she made it a living reality. "I never tried to do this before," she said; and one knew that hereafter her "normal" clients would benefit from her sharpened perceptions and better organization.

The worst frustration of all, though, if I may come back to a recurring theme in these letters, is to be treated as though you are invisible or—at best—totally stupid. The only defense is, I suppose, to try to see the humor of such situations and to remember that this is not a French attitude or a Canadian one or a West Indian but a universal problem.

One of the favorite stories in our family, you know, is about the time your mother and I took a bus tour in Scotland. At our lunch stop we were the last people off the bus, as usual; and by the time we got into the little country tea room, we had to be seated at separate tables. My table mates were a very reserved British family who acknowledged my arrival with a faint, frosty smile and a nod of the head. We sat there in uncomfortable silence until the waitress brought their first course. The look of horror on her face was undisguised as she turned to the lady at the table and asked, "Will he have soup?" The lady drew herself up as only British ladies are capable of doing and icily replied, "I haven't any notion—*he's* not with us."

To this day, when I run into such treatment, it helps me to remember that quite hilarious experience.

But cost and physical barriers and stupid people and occasional frustration are insignificant burdens to bear in comparison to the rewards. Travel has always been considered "broadening," but I think it has had special liberating dimensions for me. Let me see if I can spell that out a bit.

At the most superficial level, travel has produced great satisfaction in enabling me to see places previously only read or dreamed about. However skillful television—even in "living color"—may be in bringing visual images of far-off places into your life, it cannot hope to duplicate even a fraction of the excitement of being there in person. It is not only that the presence of television cameras injects an artificial, distorting element into every situation so that the event or the place or even the people involved become the creature of the medium. Even television at its best cannot reproduce the feel, the smells, the spirit of a setting because these are all very dynamic and must be experienced firsthand. There is absolutely no comparison between seeing a TV documentary and actually lurching across the rough terrain of the Ngorongoro Crater in a Land Rover in pursuit of rhinos and elephants and lions and a hundred other preposterously unique animals. No travelogue can capture the drama and excitement one feels at the Pyramids in the moonlight, or of being caught up in the celebrating crowd of Parisians the night General de Gaulle was defeated at the polls and resigned, or of driving down a lush tropical road in Jamaica and have hostile natives shake their fists at you and yell, "White man shall die!" You have to be really there to know how these things feel.

And it is the experience of being there, I suppose, that makes *you* suddenly feel different. You find yourself saying, "I'm just like other people." Whatever your limitations in fact, whatever your conditioning in thinking about yourself as less than a whole person, you now realize that some of the barriers to "normal" activity never really existed at all. You, like countless other people, are treading on ground where great men have lived and great events have been played out; and the satisfaction of reliving the past and anticipating the future is no longer just vicarious.

Even that discovery about oneself is secondary to what he learns about the "stranger."

The handicapped person can fairly well structure and program his usual existence to minimize his dependence upon others. His life can more or less be routinized so that his well-being needs to be entrusted only to the few who have been confirmed as being trustworthy.

Whenever one decides to travel, especially when one decides to do it alone, a whole host of threatening possibilities arises. The human distrust of strangers goes very deep. We readily assume that the "foreign" and the "foreigner" are dangerous and to be suspected because we have no experience on which to base another kind of judgment. We cling to the contradictory notions that the foreigner is inferior because he does not know our enlightened practices and beliefs, while at the same time assuming that he is clever enough to cheat us almost at will. Even if one can rationalize these irrational feelings, the handicapped person still has to deal with the very real fact that he must accept help from people with no prior knowledge about their competency or their good will. In other countries, this is generally compounded by the necessity of frequently communicating with people in even less reliable forms than language.

It is a liberating discovery to find that whatever differences there are among men, we all really share in a common humanity. People are much the same everywhere. If one understands that our differences are still on a human spectrum of experience and not radical discontinuities, one can begin to find points of contact on which to develop relationship. One finds that some people everywhere are cruel and exploitative, others are hostile and threatening, and still others are insensitive and unkind. One quickly perceives that some are willing to be helpful only because of the rewards they expect to gain.

But one also finds that most people everywhere are basically decent, compassionate, willing, interested, and interesting. They may appear aloof or unconcerned, but that may only mean that you, too, are a stranger. I have found that in ninety-nine out of every one hundred instances a request for help is met with serious effort to give it. Sometimes the exuberance of willingness can be frightening, as it was in West Africa several times when— confronted by steps—I would find myself hoisted up by so many eager hands that I expected all of us to fall into a mass of tangled arms and legs!

Generalized willingness to be of help is only a part of the story. There are many who voluntarily go beyond the call of courtesy because they genuinely want you to have a richer experience. I remember an early trip to Washington, for example, when I was met by my college friend Rollie Hultsch. We went to the Lincoln Memorial and I sat raptly at the foot of those dozens of steps, gazing at the distant but still very awing statue. Hultsch knew of my interest in American history and the particular regard I had for Abraham Lincoln. So, much to my surprise, he said, "Let's go up." He pulled me up all those marble stairs so that, at last, I could sit beneath the great brooding figure. "Why did you do it?" I asked him afterward. "I just thought you should have the chance to see Lincoln the way everybody else did." I would have settled for less, but Rollie wanted me to have more.

And that is the way it has been over and over. You remember Chaim, one of the guides we had in Israel. I expressed my disappointment to him at being unable to see any of Old Jerusalem. He asked why I had not gone and responded, when I told him of the position taken by the previous day's guide, "It's difficult, to be sure, but not impossible." So off we all went, bumping down those narrow streets with steps at frequent intervals until at last we came to the Church of the Holy Sepulchre. And yet I could not be too upset with Abraham because he, too, had exerted himself by showing me through the many levels of the National Museum the day before.

You have already experienced this "over and above" spirit, too. Do you remember how Don Campbell tucked you—cast and all—under his strong right arm and used his left to steady you both as he climbed down into a visiting Australian submarine in Bermuda a few years ago? And I know you remember how Keith Johnston, our handsome young guide in Ireland, carried you to the top of Blarney Castle so you could kiss the stone—even though we all agreed that you could teach it some lessons in eloquence!

Then there was another incident in which you shared. We have joked a lot about our visit to the Green Grotto in Jamaica a couple of years ago. Brad Rentzel was with us, you know, and he had enquired at the entrance about how difficult it would be for us to explore the cave. He came back with the word that there were a total of fifty-five steps. It was agreed that this sounded possible if difficult, and off we set. What we did not learn until it was too late was that the fifty-five steps were in flights of varying numbers separated by all kinds of obstacles like huge boulders, very irregular terrain, even one spot where one had to bend practically double in order to get through a small opening in the rock.

Somehow we made it through intact. Your mother carried you much of the way; occasionally there was no choice but for you to ease yourself down steps or across fallen tree trunks. Brad tested every muscle and sinew in keeping me upright much of the way; but I, too, had to slither across the ground on the seat of my pants. Rashly, foolishly, dangerously we all persisted even though each turn in the path seemed to bring an obstacle even more difficult to overcome than the last. Finally the grotto was reached and we floated in the small boat, more grateful for a respite from our efforts than for the fascinating details of the cavern. Then we struggled on until finally we were back at the entrance. In a combination of exhilaration and exhaustion, we toasted one another and our collective triumph with our cool drinks. Brad and I thumped each other's shoulders in a mute yet eloquent affirmation of an event of human solidarity which immeasurably deepened an already warm friendship.

Human solidarity—maybe that is the liberating lesson travel has taught me. It has been experienced in so many places. In Scotland—where, when my chair broke down and was quickly repaired in "the best garage" of the tiny village of Kyle of Lochalsh (sp?), money was refused and my protestations of having been a bother were brushed aside with the comment, "It's been no bother. You're in Scotland now!" And in Nairobi—where our guide of several days on "safari," Harris Kariuki, insisted on taking us home to meet his family and was only slightly abashed by his wife's obvious distress at having unexpected company. And in London—where a woman passer-by brightened the usual overcast day with the admiring comment as I bounced my chair up a curb, "Brave man—it's men like you that keep the Empire going!" And in Chicago—where, after the disastrous Democratic Convention of 1968, a policeman politely asked if he could help me across a busy intersection and I commented to your mother, "I guess I can't call him a fascist pig now!" And in all those other places, Polly, where people have reached out to us spontaneously with gestures of friendliness and concern.

Over and over again we have experienced acts of grace. I cannot find any other terminology which better describes them. In them gulfs between men of different nations and cultures and races have been bridged, common things affirmed, fear replaced by celebration of an essential unity. Who could now persuade us, Polly, to subscribe to the lingering myths of men which seek to reduce the stranger to something evil and dangerous and defiling? For we have met the stranger and have found him, potentially at least, to be our brother.

I guess these experiences have made me forever impatient with all expressions of ghetto mentality. One can affirm, I think, the strengths of his own race and culture without locking it behind walls of exclusion and suspicion. I have occasionally been attacked for being disloyal to the particular subculture of which I am by definition a part. I take this as fair criticism. I have not always avoided playing the "nigger" game of feeling there was something disgraceful about being what I am and of denying my clear identity as a handicapped person. I acknowledge that I have not always been responsible in promoting the welfare of my own kind. And yet no one can persuade me that the world or I would be better off if I were to imprison myself in militant handicapism. The time probably will come in the predictably unpredictable days when I shall be out in the streets shouting "gimp power," but it will only be because handicapped folk are rightly demanding recognition of who they are as well as what they are.

None of us is free, it seems to me, until all of us are free to cross the boundaries, back and forth, able—in St. Paul's term—to be "all things to all men" in that we feel at home in any setting because we are, whatever the differences, always among "our own kind."

A final couple of anecdotes.

When I was six or seven I had a truly spectacular Christmas. All of them were memorable, since—as you do now—I received many gifts, including some from people who really had no particular reason to give them. But this

Christmas was something special. I had received a toy gasoline station, a farm set, a doll house, a silver mechanical pencil, books—just lots and lots of things. When Aunt Lida arrived for Christmas dinner, while she was still in an adjoining room, I shouted to her, "Aunt Lida, come and see what I got. I got—" There was an instant's hesitation; what superlative could I possibly find that would do justice to the reality? "I got—the whole world!"

That's the way I feel now. After the privilege of going many places and coming to know many, many people, "I got the whole world."

You remember what happened to me in Nigeria in 1968 when that wonderful country was split down the middle by the tragic civil war. I had asked the Nigerian mission at the United Nations for advice about people I should see in order to learn about Nigerian approaches to urban problems. Minutes after I arrived in Lagos a representative of the Ministry of Information arrived with a schedule of appointments the government had already made on my behalf. The first was with Chief Omo Bare, the Commissioner of Rehabilitation, the government minister reponsible for the rebuilding of the "liberated areas."

I still do not know why the Nigerian government elected to use that visit as the occasion for announcing a general amnesty for the rebels. Cameramen kept circling around as Chief Omo Bare and I talked; and that night some of the film was on television, while next day pictures were plastered across the front pages of the newspapers and my name was repeated on every newscast on radio. Generously, I was referred to as "a prominent Harlem clergyman"! The upshot of all this was that I became an instant celebrity: everywhere I went after that people would stop me to say they had seen my picture and wanted to welcome me to their country.

I wanted to visit the University of Ibadan, about a

hundred miles away. Since most of the equipment on Air Nigeria and the railroad had been commandeered for war purposes and service on both was irregular and unreliable, it was recommended that I hire a car for the trip. I felt very important sitting in splendor in the back seat, while my impressive driver threaded his way through the dense traffic of buses and "lorries" and donkey carts and bicycles. Every few miles there was a military check point. Generally we were waved on through, but just outside Ibadan a young soldier cradling a machine gun ordered us to the side of the road. "I want to inspect your boot," he told the driver. As far as I knew there was nothing in the car trunk except my wheelchair. Still my driver made no effort to leave his seat. Instead he blandly looked at the soldier and said, "But you don't understand. This man is an ambassador." Flustered, the soldier expressed profuse apologies and motioned that we should go on.

The American Embassy in Lagos would have been much surprised to learn of my new rank, I feel sure. Yet maybe I was a kind of ambassador, helping to prepare the way for other handicapped people to overcome their fears and to set forth with some confidence to explore far-off places. Beyond that, I would like to think that when people like you and me travel around this nation and this world, we somehow are saying that we are ambassadors carrying the message that this is one world, with one humanity, under the one ultimate reality, who is "God and Father of us all."

I'll write you again soon, Sweetie.

Daddy

Education

4

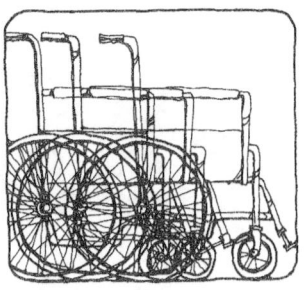

Dear Polly

A few years ago I was asked to be a character witness at the trial of a young man accused of resisting arrest. In the case tried before his a black clergyman whom I knew fairly well was sworn in to be a similar kind of witness. He gave his name and his church affiliation, but before the defense attorney could ask anything else, the judge—a chronically nasty man popularly known as "the Nazi"—leaned forward and asked, "Tell me, Reverend, where did you go to school?"

One did not need to be an expert in racism to know the import of the question. If my friend had had to acknowledge, as so many of his peers would have to do, that he had barely finished grade or high school much less gone to recognized "institutions of higher learning," his testimony would have been discounted if not discredited in the minds of the judge and most of the spectators. As it happened, this minister had several degrees from quite reputable schools and the subject of educational qualifications was quickly dropped.

Then it was my turn. The defense attorney asked me to identify myself. As an afterthought, I turned to face the justice and said that I was a graduate of Wabash College and Union Theological Seminary— "or aren't you interested in *my* academic credentials?" The judge and I glared at each other, and then the testimony continued. (We won the case, incidentally, but only because "the Nazi" was outvoted by his colleagues on the three-man bench!)

Afterward I got to thinking about the implications of

what had taken place. If it was unexpected that the black minister had "proper education," it could be no less for me. For when I was a child the State of Indiana assumed no responsibility for the education of the "homebound." Repeatedly my family pleaded with local school officials for some assistance, such as tutoring, but with no success. To be sure, the county superintendent of schools was sympathetic; at least he volunteered to give occasional advice on teaching techniques to my mother, who was determined that I was going to have a good education, and for years he kept me supplied with sample textbooks.

I still remember the homemade "flash cards" on which my mother had drawn the alphabet and then words of increasing difficulty. Apparently I learned to read easily, and from then to the present my consumption of the printed word has been enormous and varied. Twice a week during my childhood my grandfather would go to the small town library to get a new supply of books. Fortunately the librarian had some imagination, so the "exciting" books of such people as Rafael Sabatini and Zane Grey were mixed in with duller fare.

I had a facile mind and a very retentive memory even as a child, and my interests ranged widely. I loved geography, and at one point I could have told you the location of every obscure peninsula and the height of even secondary mountains anywhere in the world. Occasionally you are still impressed with my knowledge of such facts.

Even though we lived on a farm, I was not totally cut off from the world. We subscribed to a daily as well as weekly newspapers, and we had a battery-powered radio. I was restricted to six hours' listening each day. That was enough to cram in soap operas, comedy, drama, and—one of my favorite categories, oddly enough—news. I still remember hearing the broadcast about the destruction of the Hindenberg, the great German "blimp," and I listened attentively to the speeches and the commentaries during those years when the world moved irresistibly toward war.

At one point I wanted desperately to be a diplomat so that I, too, could take part in all those exciting events. I even went so far as to write the State Department about the qualifications one needed to be in the diplomatic service. Apparently two good legs was one of the foremost requirements. Anyway, that did not stop me from writing letters to diplomats from other nations in Washington for information about many things. Surprisingly, some of them entered into correspondence with me. Walter Nash continued to send me Christmas cards after he returned to New Zealand, for a time even after he became prime minister. My favorite of all was Henrik de Kauffman of Denmark who looked and acted the way I thought an ambassador should. I admired his courage in breaking with his government and leading Iceland and Greenland into the war against Germany. It was a thrill in later years to visit him twice in Washington.

And as my letter writing became more proficient and daring, I wrote to other people. Wendell Willkie was one of my boyhood heroes, and I have still a number of letters from him, one beginning with an acknowledgment of mine telling him how impressed I was with his book *One World*.

I did so much reading and radio listening in those early years that I became "educated" without even knowing it. That is, I had accumulated a vast fund of "facts" about many things. One day someone said to my mother that I should get official recognition for all the work I had done. That set me to thinking. Why not, indeed? So I wrote another letter, this time to my old friend Don Crist, the superintendent of schools. He confessed to me later that this letter threw him into a panic. He did not want to discourage or disappoint me, but he could see no way of acceding to my request. So, like any good bureaucrat does, he indulged in a bit of buck passing: he wrote to his counterpart on the state level and dumped the problem into his lap. The reply neatly passed the problem back to Crist: there was no law or regulation to prevent his authorizing a high-school diploma, but he would have to determine the means for justifying such an action.

What I finally did was to take comprehensive examinations in every grade- and high-school subject. Grade school was a snap; that took only an afternoon of writing. High school took a year and a half of intensive study. Important people rallied to my support. Cousin Doris Lackey was a member of the State Board of Education that year, and she saw to it that I was provided both with encouragement and copies of all standard texts. But the real heroine of the story was Bertha Bostick.

"Bert" was assistant principal and English teacher at the Monon High School. She had been there, as the kids described it, "forever and ever." She epitomized, I suppose, those legendary characteristics of the dedicated, self-sacrificing teacher. Some thought her dull, out-of-date, something of a martinet. Others—of whom I quickly became one—considered her to be an exciting teacher, a compassionate human being, and a loyal friend. This woman was assigned to help me negotiate the maze to a high-school diploma. For the next year and a half she came out to our country home at least once a week. Not only did she monitor my examinations, but she also helped me establish study patterns, arranged for tutoring when that was needed (as in math), and in general served as cheer leader when I got discouraged about ever completing the process.

Maybe even more important, Bert was determined to broaden my contacts with my peers in the school. Some of the students were encouraged to visit me. I was invited to contribute a regular column to the school newspaper and was elected to honorary membership in a boys' club. As the formal relationship drew to a close, she engineered invitations and made the necessary arrangements to enable me to attend some school functions, like the senior prom. We both were disappointed when the principal ruled against my participation in the graduation exercises because there was still an incomplete subject. When, a few weeks later, my "special order" diploma was delivered, it is hard to say whether Bert or I was most proud.

In the normal course of events the story would have ended there, but actually Bert's most crucial contribution to my education was still to come. I have already told you about the grim day when the doctors acknowledged that I would never walk and virtually forbade me to become more active physically. Like Charles McCarty, Bert Bostick anxiously awaited the outcome of those examinations. Her emotional involvement was less obvious but, I suspect, equally as great. I remember vividly her visit that momentous week as I recited the disappointing news. After a time, she quietly said, "When are you going to college?" My response was one of shock; had she heard nothing that I had said, not noted the authoritative judgments of the doctors which precluded my doing anything of the kind? "Yes, I know what they said. But I repeat my question, 'When are you going to college?' " What could have been more unlikely —a woman steeped for so many years in the authoritarianism of the educational system daring to defy an even more rigorous structure of authority! She knew I wanted to go, that I should go, that indeed I had to go if I were not— figuratively at least—to die. Her encouragement was decisive, and I shall always be very grateful to her.

There were still substantial hurdles to overcome. Letters went to every college in Indiana asking about the feasibility of my applying for admission. Every one of them, with one exception, responded negatively. Many cited the vastly increased enrollments occasioned by the end of World War II and the beginning of the "GI Bill of Rights." Most honestly acknowledged that they had never had a student in a wheelchair, envisioned serious problems, and would not consider accepting me.

The one exception was Wabash College, a small all-male school at Crawfordsville. Their reply recited much of the above, but ended with the assurance that serious consideration would be given before they reached a decision one way or the other. In a few weeks the director of admissions came to see me, and later I was asked to visit the campus. I don't think I have ever been so scared in my life as the day I was ushered into the presence of the president, the dean of the faculty, the director of admissions, the professor of psychology, the chairman of the science division, and a few others who never really got identified. They grilled me for over an hour, asking me in minute detail how I would take care of myself, how I would get to classes, how I would expect to do a thousand necessary things. Then the conversation suddenly shifted. It was almost as though I were no longer there. They began to discuss among themselves how and whether they could make the necessary adjustments to make my coming possible. It became clearer by the minute that they were really on my side and were doing their best to come up with an affirmative answer.

And they did. From that point on the college was committed to doing whatever was necessary to make my stay as happy and as productive as possible. "Fergie" Ormes grumbled a lot, but found the money to build a ramp to the dorm. Harry Cotton, my beloved professor of philosophy, sweated and strained to pull me up a long flight of stairs to his second-floor classroom—and the next day the school adopted the policy that classes would be shifted to ground floor rooms as necessary. "Briggie"—W. Norwood Brigance, the speech professor—excused me from the required courses (which met in the third-floor studios) and quietly offered to coach me personally as needed. By the end of the first semester there was hardly a professor or a student who had not hoisted me up some steps or in other ways become a part of what had become a genuine all-college project.

I have to admit, Polly, that despite an I.Q. of 132, I was an indifferent student. My grade average was respectable, but hardly sensational. It is not for that reason that Wabash was a liberating experience. I was permitted for the first time in my life to do what I wanted—and most of all I wanted to become a fully socialized human being. No one had more friends, no one was readier to drop the books and talk or play chess or to walk downtown for a milkshake. Acceptance by the college community seemed to come quickly and soon nicknames were applied: very early I gained the title of "The Mechanized Monster"; after it became known that I planned to study for the ministry, I became known as "The Holy Roller"! Another sign of my acceptance was that I did not completely escape the hazing newcomers always experience. On one occasion I was even dumped into a snowbank because my friends said I was getting too "uppity"!

Dr. Cotton told me that in his letter of recommendation to Union Seminary he recounted an episode in my career which apparently had impressed the college community far more than it had me. The first fall the long-time rivalry between Wabash and DePauw—another school about thirty miles away—had been revived after the wartime truce. Every night for about two weeks before the annual football game, bands of students would invade each other's campus to paint signs on buildings or to apply the opposing school's colors to some important landmark, like the founder's statue. Ostensibly because of my age—I was twenty-one and therefore excused from "childish" things—I was told I need not take part in the guard duty that was instituted as the rivalry became more intense and the vandalism more outrageous. An alarm was sounded late one evening and everyone left the dorm to take up his assigned position. I fumed for a time in that deserted building, then dressed and armed myself with a baseball bat I found in the hallway. Everything seemed to be quiet on campus and I had almost decided to return to my bed when, suddenly, car lights appeared and the vehicle swiftly bore down on the lovely old house where the president lived. Agonized by the thought that blue paint might be smeared across that white facade, I sped toward the "enemy." I arrived just as the president and his wife emerged from the car and looked a bit startled by this apparition brandishing a baseball bat! I quickly mumbled an explanation and fled.

Through those four years at Wabash there were times when I resented the demands that were put upon me. After all, couldn't they *see* that I was crippled? Surely some concessions should be made beyond my being excused from guard duty and gym classes. There were other times, though, when I was convinced that things were being made too easy for me, that people were really pampering me; and I resented this just as much. Indeed, in later years, a wise and understanding psychiatrist helped me articulate what I guess I had felt all along, namely, that I felt I had to be better at everything than anyone else, and the impossibility of this was sometimes more than I could bear.

As it turned out, the doctors were at least partly right. I did have more fractures, and these interfered from time to time with my school work. (I was a bit shaken after one such episode to turn on the local radio station and hear that I was in "fair condition" at the hospital!) The most serious was the four months' hospitalization in New York which cut out the end of the first semester and the beginning of the second. Only a part of the year's work could realistically be completed; and I began my senior year with the almost overwhelming burden of having to pass forty-five hours of class work if I expected to graduate on schedule. Somehow it happened. Courses were completed, papers written, exams taken. And finally the day came when my name was called, the students stood, and the president and dean came down the steps from the podium to confer a degree and their best wishes.

On that day of triumph I foolishly allowed myself to assume that the big hurdles had now been overcome. Now, surely, there would be no problem about getting into a seminary; surely there would now be no reluctance to employ my skills. The reality of our existence, Polly, is that in some areas—perhaps even in most—we win many battles, but never the war. So I experienced a whole new round of letters of rejection as I applied to graduate schools. It seemed to cut no ice that I had successfully completed college; in their eyes I was still essentially a "problem."

You have, unhappily, already run into this in your young life. For what we had considered wise and rational reasons, your mother and I agreed from the outset that we did not want you to go to a school for crippled children. Your disability did not seem of such severity and limitation that you needed such special treatment and protection. We were determined that you were going to make your way in the "normal" world with as few detours and sidetracks as possible. (That automatically eliminated the public schools, since they would insist on your going to a "special" school. Our decision, then, meant making some economic sacrifices to keep you in private schools.)

So while we were grateful for the Philanthropic League's good treatment of you in their special nursery school and were flattered by the invitation to enroll you in a "demonstration" class at Teachers College one summer, we rejoiced that Riverside Church Nursery School accepted you and that there seemed to be no undue problem in getting you enrolled in first grade at St. Hilda's and St. Hugh's, a very good Episcopal private school. That year seemed to be a great success from all standpoints; you loved the school and everyone at the school seemed to love you.

You can imagine our shock, then, after having signed the new contract and having sent in our deposit for your second year to receive a letter from Reverend Mother Ruth saying you would not be permitted to return for "reasons too painful to write and too painful to read." She refused either to see or to talk with me until your mother had hysterics in the presence of the bishop, and he intervened on our behalf. That interview was one of the most bizarre I have ever been through. I was told by that imperious old woman that she would terminate the conversation immediately if I attempted to make any notes. So we fenced with each other for a time, reviewing the various areas where you might increasingly have difficulty as you grew older—things like getting to the public toilets. She vehemently denied my charge that she was scared something would happen to you on school property and we would sue the school for a lot of money. My offer to sign any kind of waiver their attorney might draw up was quickly spurned. Finally I asked about the "painful" matters referred to in her letter and was amazed to learn that we had been talking about them all along. Apparently her Victorian sensibilities were overwhelmed when we had to consider the problems of going to the bathroom.

In time, a temporary resolution was reached when Reverend Mother agreed to let you come one more year if Mummy would work at the school and get you to the bathroom, lunch, etc. But for a long while gloom hung heavy in our household as we found no way out for that year. Somehow we managed to keep all this from you until one day when your mother and Reverend Mother had a brief encounter at school. "It's about me, isn't it?" you said when you thought Mummy was being evasive. She decided to tell you the facts. Your little face was very troubled that night when I got home. "They don't want me at St. Hilda's," you said. It was your first real experience of rejection.

Ironically, Dalton School—where you now go and which could not be more secular—has been infinitely more courageous, understanding, and innovative than the institution which stresses "Christian" foundations. Even though you have had a disastrous year physically, you have managed to keep up with your studies; and at no point has anyone at Dalton suggested you were a problem to be dealt with by being asked to leave.

Anyway, to get back to my own narrative, there was one ray of hope—a long letter from President Van Dusen of Union Theological Seminary, describing what seemed to him to be major physical barriers, said that they were willing to pursue the subject of my coming if I wished. He was rather overwhelmed, I think, when I arrived for a visit. "How did you get here?" he asked. "By Greyhound bus," I replied. The word ultimately came that Union was willing to risk it whenever I felt I was ready to come. Yet, when I wrote of my readiness, the school seemed to have second thoughts and tried to encourage me to stay on at Butler School of Religion in Indianapolis where I had already taken a few courses. But by now I was determined—and you know full well how immovably stubborn I can be—and I left for New York not knowing whether I would be permitted to enroll.

It all worked out, as you know. Everyone at Union—students and faculty alike—rallied round to make the experience a success. History repeated itself in that I still was not free of periods of feeling sorry for myself and others when I flagellated myself for my stupidity and slothfulness. Despite this—and marathons of bridge playing—courses were somehow completed, papers written, exams taken; and then another day of satisfaction when another president came down the steps to wish me well.

I have accumulated still another degree since, and you know how scandalized some people get when I say that degrees are really of little consequence, that they have no necessary relationship to education. I guess what I mean by this is that schools and schooling are only a means to an end, not the end. To be educated, I have come to understand, has very little to do with facts and their memorization. It does not even have much to do with one's ability to be molded in the image of his "teacher."

What has been important in making the educational process liberating for me? As far as I can sort it out, the first thing I would have to mention is the ability to read well. I am scandalized that this is not at the top of every educator's priority list. I am cheered because you do read well, even though you find very little yet that you consider worth reading.

I keenly felt the embarrassment of the kids at Chambers Church when they were asked to read something and would stumble uncomprehendingly through even the simplest words. The arguments that some well-meaning people use these days to excuse our increasing level of semi-literacy strike me as "cop-outs." To be sure, some illiterate people have "made it big" in this world, relying on lettered aides to do their reading and writing. I have often served in that role myself; I once used the analogy of the gangster's lawyer—the "mouthpiece"—to describe the function I still play for the Triangle, for example: translating their thoughts and ideas into language other people can read and understand. And I spent a lot of time, as you know, reading reports and other material so that the Triangle people can keep abreast of what thoughts and ideas others have. But it would be better, in terms both of practicality and personal satisfaction, if they could do it for themselves.

Then there are those who say that we are in a "post-literate" age, when television and other forms of communication have replaced the written word. The most I am willing to concede is that they have "supplemented" the written word. The ancient Chinese sage certainly was dealing with reality when he claimed superiority for pictures over words. What he did not say in necessary qualification, not being—as we are—bombarded with constant visual images from a variety of screens, was that this depends upon the quality of the picture. While television has marvelous capacities to inform, it also has great capacity to bore and to confuse. At its best, television may be able to deal with a subject only fragmentarily.

Our chief contact with both the past and with evocative language—language that stirs and arouses all kinds of intellectual and visceral responses—will for a long time continue to be through the printed page. We can and must learn from the past, while not being bound by it. The lessons of history are learned only when they are tested, and revalidated, if you will, in contemporary experience.

But most of all I covet for you the joy I have had in reading voraciously across the accumulated literary riches of mankind, the joy of slipping away to a quiet spot and savoring beautiful language and reflecting on its meaning. There is even joy in seeing a word for the first time and having your curiosity piqued to the extent that you look it up in a good dictionary and then make it a part of your own vocabulary. The Anglo-Saxonisms that have come into renewed popularity in the speech of the last decade do indeed communicate, but there is much more that man can and has to say.

The ability to read well and familiarity with some of the world's literary riches, however, is not the end of the educational quest, but perhaps only its beginning. Possibly the best learning takes place in dialogue with other human beings. There is so much to learn, and so much of what there is to learn is not even verbal. But the meaning of our existence is somehow bound up in the quality of human relationships we experience and to which we contribute. It is in human interaction that we begin to learn that there is always a whole world of feeling and knowing that is still beyond facts.

I am not being flippant when I say that most of the

learning that occurred when I was in college or seminary took place outside the classroom and beyond the reading of books. What my generation called "bull sessions" and a more recent one "rap sessions" are a necessary tool in testing oneself against others emotionally and intellectually. Through this process one finds certain people who are especially compatible companions in the learning quest, not because your ideas necessarily correspond but because you both are excited about examining new ideas and pushing each other really to wrestle with these ideas.

I guess I am almost at the point of saying that the best learning takes place through such "picking of brains." Maybe the truest sign of educational development is a growing skill in asking questions. And one discovers how his life is constantly enriched as he is exposed to as diverse a representation of humanity as possible; everyone can tell us something interesting and useful to know.

One implication of this is that one's education is never completed but is always in process. There is always more to know; and to remain open and curious and alert is, it seems to me, to remain alive. It is risky, of course, because it means that one must be willing to have all his assumptions as to truth subjected to repeated tests. The truth of the matter, however, is that we must make judgments and take positions always on the basis of partial knowledge. Today's truth is always subject to tomorrow's additional evidence. And most of that evidence will be mediated through people, as you are exposed to new data, new insights, new perspectives.

Most of the world's troubles are caused by our dogged clinging to questionable assumptions. Most of the positions we hold are tagged with the addendum "and that's a fact"—you know, assumptions like "all blacks are inferior," "all whites are racists," "all handicapped persons are mentally incompetent." To share ideas, to analyze them, to explore their social implications—all this is involved in education.

The ability to do these things is a characteristic of our humanity. How well we do them determines whether our humanity ends up being humane or inhumane.

I recently went back to Wabash, as you know. Now that I had achieved a slight degree of fame as an author, they invited me to give a morning chapel talk and an evening lecture. It had been suggested that for the former I should tell what had happened to me since I graduated nearly twenty years ago. I decided that it was an impossibility to crowd all the significant events into a fifteen- or eighteen-minute speech. Instead I elected to make some comments about what Wabash had done for me in those four interesting years. The first, I said, was to introduce me to some people who were racially, culturally, and ideologically different from me. The second was to introduce me to a whole world of new ideas. The third was to help me be unafraid of both.

That is the kind of educational liberation I wish for you.

As always, with all my love, Polly.

Daddy

Freedom

5

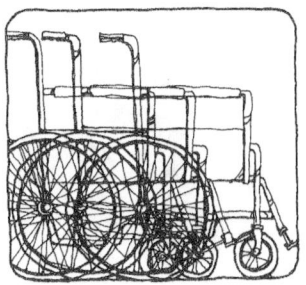

Dear Polly

One day, not too long ago, you will remember, we were lined up at the entrance to the Hospital for Special Surgery, waiting to unload you for a cast change. Two cars ahead someone was helping a child into a wheelchair. A taxi crowded alongside of us, as New York taxis are wont to do; and spurred by the honking of the car behind him the cab driver began leaning on his own horn. I knew he could not possibly see what was causing the blockage, but then ignorance has never been a deterrent to action. After a few seconds, I could stand it no longer and said to the taxi driver, "Do you want him to run down the child in the wheelchair?" At first there was blaming of the driver in the rear; when I pointed out he had been blowing his horn as well, the taxi driver's mood turned nasty and he snarled at me, "Mind your own g.d. business." There were a few other exchanges of equally pleasant nature. Then the car in front began to move. "Well, are you going or am I?" the taxi driver shouted. "After you," I replied; "I'm unloading a wheelchair, and it would upset me if you blew your horn at me."

As you well know, one dynamic operating in this little episode of life in the great city was the long-standing feud I have had with New York taxi drivers. While there are notable exceptions—like the driver who picked me up at the hospital most Sunday mornings for five years when I was doing services there as well as at Chambers and would regularly bring me containers of coffee, even a ham sandwich one Easter Sunday when he was afraid I had had no chance to get breakfast—many cab drivers are surly, attempt to overcharge you, and usually do not want to go to the sections of New York that we frequent.

    We also know well how many "blind" drivers there are—those who will swear on their mother's grave they did not see us waving to them, although they can spot other potential passengers a quarter of a mile away; or the super-safe drivers—those who cannot possibly change traffic lanes to pick *us* up, although they can careen across a whole avenue for others. It was only recently that a cab driver refused to give your mother change because she was rude enough to tell him that a charge for the use of his trunk for your wheelchair was against Police Department regulations. We know all the regulations because we long ago decided to fight back and report negligent taxi drivers, even if it did mean an expensive trip to the Hack Bureau and perhaps a long wait to testify.

    Anyway, after that encounter at the hospital, I got to thinking about the taxi driver's demand that I mind my own business. It is not the first time people have told me that. I need not tell you that your father can be a testy, temperamental, stubborn man who is willing to take on the whole world rather than retreat if he thinks someone is trying to push him around. And, looking back over my life, it would appear that I have frequently made things my business because I thought people were being treated unjustly and that systems needed to be changed in order that society might be "humanized."

    Like, for example, when Local 1199 called their strike against New York City hospitals a few years ago. We, more than most families, are aware of skyrocketing costs of medical care. The economic argument lay behind all the pressures that were brought to bear on the striking workers. While the rhetoric was about the right of hospital patients not to be inconvenienced or endangered, the real issue was that an increase in pay to hospital workers (the union was striving for a $100-per-week minimum) would raise patient costs substantially higher. Implicit in the argument seemed to be the assumption that it was appropriate for medical costs to be subsidized by the part of the hospital staff least able to afford it—not the doctors or the administrators, but the porters and maids and kitchen helpers.

There were those who warned me that I should mind my own business then. After all, I was at that point a hospital chaplain; what was to prevent an irate administrator from firing me? More importantly, the vulnerable Schoonover family needed access to expensive medical facilities more frequently than most. It was to our self-interest not to raise embarrassing questions about how the hospital we used most treated its staff. Nonetheless, I joined a small group of New York clergy in a statement supporting the strikers in the most unambiguous terms. No doubt the outcome of the strike would have been the same in any event (the workers won their demands), but perhaps this gesture played some small role in getting them a fair settlement.

Then there was the time my name appeared in connection with an even more controversial statement. In trying to get help for Chambers parishioners with one or another of their problems, I had been fairly close to the operations of several governmental agencies. I was convinced that the City administration was not only fiscally bankrupt, but morally and psychologically as well. The mayor made a career of postponing hard decisions and of acting as though the city had no serious problems. His "tour" of riot-ravaged Harlem in a limousine with drawn curtains was appropriately symbolic of his "see no evil" approach to government. Yet he had already served twelve years in the office and the political "experts" thought it virtually certain that he would be reelected handily because no one of competence or character seemed to want the job.

And then Congressman William Fitts Ryan was persuaded to consider running in the Democratic primary. To spur him on, a group of us "radical" clergymen issued what *The Christian Century* called "an unprecedented" statement denouncing the incumbent administration and urging Mr. Ryan's ultimate election as mayor. That, too, was done despite counsels of prudence from those who said that Chambers Church would never get another "favor" from a city department. (I should add the footnote that, while Congressman Ryan did not get the nomination, the mayor decided not to run for reelection.)

That was the same argument I got on another occasion, when political passions were heightened. I agreed to run against the neighborhood's political "boss" for the State Assembly. A more politically inept movement you cannot imagine. We were easily infiltrated by the "enemy" and our most important secrets were known by them as they were known to me. The politically ambitious black man who had pleaded with me to lead the "reform movement" defected very early when a City job was suddenly offered to him. A "slip of the tongue" in testimony in court when we were desperately defending our nominating petitions against challenge resulted in an unfavorable decision and our losing nearly everything. It was clear that our club member had "sold out." And so on. Around all this turmoil raged a small-scale debate whether it was proper for a clergyman to be mixed up in "this dirty business of politics." My opponent clearly did not think so; he was almost apoplectic when we accidentally met at the elevator at the Board of Elections. "Of all people," he spluttered, "I would never have expected this of you."

My foray into politics was not without a few benefits, though. It had at least the modest effect of making our political leader more visible in the neighborhood and more responsive to local needs. It was no particular strain to write him a congratulatory note when he was elected head of Tammany Hall. Beyond that, a few people were encouraged to take the political process more seriously. Mainly the benefit, as far as I was concerned, was the subtle change in relationship which resulted with a number of people in the community. They were perplexed yet on the whole pleased that a "shepherd" had chosen to demonstrate in this fairly dramatic fashion his willingness to risk his own safety on behalf of his flock.

And in more recent days, as you know, I have become a more militant "peacenik." I have come to see our involvement in South Viet Nam as immoral and indefensible. In typical fashion, the consequences of that have been mixed. Who but me would be teargassed in Washington during the November 15 Moratorium demonstration? It really was quite innocent—although no one really believes it. We did not even know anything was going on at Dupont Circle that night; we did not even know we were anywhere near Dupont Circle! It is quite an experience to be teargassed, one every person should perhaps have once! With your head you know you will soon recover, but with your emotions you are sure you are about to die.

That little episode did nothing to dampen our enthusiasm for the demonstration, however. In some sense it was a profoundly religious experience. Mummy and I have told you how we marched at the outside of the line of march (I get a little nervous being in the middle of great throngs of people, unable to see what is happening around me) and therefore had a chance to chat with a lot of the young people who performed so magnificently as marshals on that very cold day. Over and over again we were warmly greeted; "How great of you to come," some said. Again and again we were offered food. I said to one young man, "Boy, a cup of hot coffee sure would taste good now." "I'm sorry I don't have any coffee," he replied, "but how about some Southern Comfort?" Another young man asked if I were warm enough and when I indicated that I really wasn't, he reached down and said, "Well, at least I can turn up your coat collar for you." And someone else gave me an impromptu back rub to help the circulation. And an obviously nearsighted young lady flung her arms around me, kissed me, and expostulated, "You're beautiful." That same kind of generosity, compassion, and commitment has been shown by America's youth a number of times in recent years on a scale that staggers the imagination. It is the kind of spirit which I think should be normative in the church. Whether it is manifested in or out of the church, I am heartened by the fact that it still exists in our nation.

I have spent all my professional life in the black ghetto. I really never intended to do that any more, I suppose, than I intended doing most of the things I have ended up doing. There were no black people anywhere near the little country town that was my home address. I am sure that my family never knew a real live black person, although I still recall hearing the male members telling blatantly racist jokes and solemnly repeating the myths about black people that white America seems to cherish even now.

I did know a black person—Catherine, who was a maid at James Whitcomb Riley Hospital in Indianapolis and who was far more likely to stop and chat with a lonely, homesick little boy than the other personnel. No one could have persuaded me even then that Catherine was inferior in any way; for my money, she was tops! Years later, when I began making frequent trips to Chicago and stayed at the Palmer House, the black doormen would greet me like a long-lost relative. A friend told me about the time a new employee at the hotel received a terrible dressing down because he had accepted a quarter from me for getting me a taxi—"We don't take tips from him," he was told.

Crawfordsville, where I went to college, had a small black ghetto which dated back many, many years. In the late 1940s, in that town which took pride in calling itself "the Athens of the Middle West," Negroes were still confined to the balcony at the local theater and no restaurant in town would serve them a meal. I was scandalized to learn that a man who attended the same church as I refused to warm a baby's bottle for a black mother who was passing through town and stopped at his coffee shop which doubled as the bus station. And Harley Cunningham, the service station operator for whom I did bookkeeping for a time, asked me seriously one summer's night if I thought he could "get away with hiring Joe for the summer?" Joe had just graduated from the town high school where he had been the star athlete. Imagine the necessity, Polly, of raising such a question! The question of whether the town's leading football player was fit to pump gas would never have been asked if Joe had not been black.

One thing led to another. I dug deeper into the relationships between black and white in that college town. I recall a long conversation with an aging female podiatrist who was the most respected leader in the black community. She poured out a tale of bitterness at how her people seemed fated forever to being "hewers of wood and drawers of water." When I asked the dean of the college why there were no black students at Wabash, he quickly assured me that it was not because of discriminatory policies but because none had recently applied.

In my senior year I decided to enter the college's oratorical contest. Everyone knew who would win; a gifted student had swept all other prizes and had been polishing his speech about the Communist take-over in China for a long time. (It was a good speech; I still remember the title—"The Bamboo Curtain"—and some of the outline.) Nonetheless I set to work putting my findings, impressions, and feelings about the status of the Negro in Crawfordsville into a speech entitled "The Shame of Athens." I said that the way this progressive college community treated its blacks was as immoral as the treatment of Socrates by another Athens. Whatever that speech lacked in technical brilliance must have been made up in passion, for I won first prize!

Then I moved to Indianapolis, where the numbers of Negroes were much greater and the "black problem," as we whites persist in calling it, was infinitely more complex. Few people seemed to be doing much to change the situation. One was a Canadian, Al Gamble, who headed a project financed by the Quakers to expand employment opportunities for blacks. It was he, for example, who persuaded the department stores to hire their first black salesmen. We both attended First Baptist Church; and I still vividly remember the tension at a Sunday evening service when one of Al's black friends came unannounced and a few of us interposed ourselves between him and some of the more racist members who threatened to "throw him out."

Indianapolis was a southern city in terms of many of its attitudes and practices. Would you believe that in 1956, when I went back there to be ordained to the ministry, my invitation of a black man to preach the sermon created a tremendous controversy? Jim Robinson was still minister of the Church of the Master then, although he had achieved an international reputation as an imaginative and courageous churchman. (It was he, incidentally, who founded Operation Cross Roads Africa—the program which sends students to many African countries each summer to work with local groups to build schools or develop special programs—which later served as the model for the Peace Corps.) When a trustee of the church learned that Jim was a Negro, he denounced me publicly as a Communist and got his colleagues to vote to refuse me use of the church building. It was only after threat of publicity in the press (it was the threat to leak this to the local Catholic newspaper which seemed to upset people the most, this being pre-John XXIII and Vatican II) by one of my supporters that the action was rescinded. The "compromise" was that I could be ordained there provided the service took place at some other time than a regularly scheduled service.

Another small blow for freedom was struck in connection with the same occasion. I went to see the manager of a leading Indianapolis restaurant to ask what was likely to happen if I entertained a distinguished black minister there for lunch. After I had assured him repeatedly that there would be only one black among a party of whites, he said, "I think we could get away with it." Jim did not stay overnight, but there would have been a similar problem with hotel accommodations.

All this controversy had been occasioned because of another of those unexpected turns of history. I think I told you in an earlier letter about what happened when Union Seminary tried to help me get a job my first year there. Since the minister at Riverside felt I was an unacceptable Sunday Church school teacher because I had not had "a normal adolescence," the field work personnel at the seminary were in a quandary about what to do with me. (At this point they still made some unwarranted assumptions about my mobility; they felt they had to place me in a position geographically close to the seminary.) One possible alternative was to assign me to work at the Church of the Master which was just down the hill in central Harlem, although some anxiety was expressed about my safety getting to and from the church. I was overjoyed with the suggestion. Maybe it was because I was curious about what life was like in a black community. Maybe I had some notion of helping to pay what I believed to be society's heavy debt to the black man. One's motives are always mixed and only partially understood. Whatever the motives, I liked being there for the most part. It would have been enough merely to have the chance to meet a man of such spiritual stature as Jim Robinson and to have the opportunity to learn how, largely through the force of personality, he had transformed a little corner of the world. I marveled at how, quietly for the most part, an oppressed people had built an institution which practiced what can only be called "practical piety." I had never known a church like that before—one which sponsored credit unions and day-care programs and a dozen other things which helped a lot of people develop a sense of their own worth.

It was an easy decision, then, to continue a relationship with black people and to go—when I graduated from seminary—to East Harlem. For a year I lived in a tiny two-room apartment on 100th Street ("the worst block in New York City") with a bathtub in the kitchen which had to be taken out because otherwise I could not even get through the door. For a year I fought rats and cockroaches, suffered the indignity of being robbed by junkies, stifled in the summer and froze in the winter. I did a lot of confused thinking in those days about "identification" with the oppressed people of that community. There were temptations to "go native"—to identify with the squalor and depravity that one saw on every side. But that, the parishioners were quick to point out whenever they were asked, did nothing to make them feel better. They wanted their ministers to identify with their hopes and dreams and aspirations for a better life, and all the concrete help they could get in making some of those hopes and dreams and aspirations become realities. It was during that year especially that I learned to respect the daily struggle people in the ghetto make merely to survive, and to admire the ability of so many to retain their sanity, their dignity, and their sense of humor.

Even then well-intentioned people outside East Harlem would ask if I did not want to move somewhere where conditions and people would be more congenial. When your mother and I were married, I confess it was a relief to move a few blocks south, across Manhattan's "Mason-Dixon Line" (96th Street), to another two-room apartment which seemed lavish in comparison to my 100th Street "home"—where there was a proper bathroom complete with tub, where there was reliable heat in winter, and where an exterminator took care of the vermin. But I rediscovered what I already knew, namely, that the people were no more congenial, perhaps less so, in this privileged community. My friends were in East Harlem, however strange that might appear to the uninitiated.

That has been your experience, too. We almost wept last year when an onlooker reported a verbal exchange between you and the girl in the next bed. Beulah Palmer had come to visit you and had stepped out to get something for you. Your roommate, you remember, asked you who Beulah was; and it is reported that your reply was, "She's just my friend." The other girl was scornful and asked, "How can a Negro be your friend?" and you answered simply, "Because she is."

Because my friends were Negroes and Puerto Ricans and a wondrously strange assortment of whites who clung to continued residence in East Harlem, it was especially poignant to leave for a time in 1958. But then the chance came to return a few months later, to become the minister at Chambers Memorial. I suppose my motives for going there were mixed, too. No doubt I wanted to "show" the skeptical denominational bureaucrats that I could successfully be the pastor of a real congregation. Perhaps

I clung to some vestiges of patronizing notions that somehow I could "help these people." But also present was the hope that maybe, together with "the saints" in that place, we could build a caring community which somehow could transcend the obvious differences among us. And I am not being profane when I say, "By God, we did!" For ten years I gave that church and that neighborhood everything I had. For ten years that church and that neighborhood nurtured me. I will spare you the familiar details—after all, if you want to know more about them, all you have to do is to read THE BOOK.

Just let me say that that decade was, for many of us, I think, a great experience of liberation. We learned, some of us, to fight among ourselves with honest if sometimes painful sharing of feeling. We championed the right of every human being to be free of unnecessary restraint, and to exercise responsibility in freedom—which, after all, is the only way it can be done. We strengthened one another in what turned out to be perpetual conflict with those forces in society which stifle human freedom. And we celebrated our modest successes. I feel no regret or shame about what happened at Chambers during those days.

The critics became more numerous as the years went by. Some people thought the Schoonovers mad for living in the midst of an increasingly turbulent community. Some thought us traitors to a society which had given us "privileges." Some expressed admiration for our "dedication," counting us somehow superhuman because we persisted in supporting what remain to this day very unpopular causes. The choices we have made have made us unacceptable to many. Occasionally I am invited to tell groups in the suburbs or out in the hinterland what it is like in the ghetto, to interpret what the events in the ghetto community mean for the whole community. Rarely am I invited a second time. With my heart I know that the black militant is right when he says that I should be working in the white community for social change, but with my head I see again how little honor any prophet has in his own home.

As attitudes and animosities have hardened in the white community, so have they in the black. One can almost graph the change in mood through the years. Our continued presence in East Harlem is an offense to some; it is not uncommon any longer to encounter undisguised hostility. There are some who rather enjoy the notion of having a few token whites around, so long as we know our "place" and are willing to "Tom" a bit on cue. But East Harlem is still home; when the time came, as I felt, to step down from the leadership of what had become a largely black institution, it was almost unthinkable that we should move.

It would be easy, perhaps safer, certainly excusable to run. But it would also be, I feel, immoral. It would be a confirmation to those on both sides of the racial divide who argue that no true communication, no genuine collaboration, no authentic human relationship is possible or desirable between black and white. I have no basis for accepting any of those premises. And so we stay on, hoping somehow that that act can become a sign of hope in the future, a gesture of human solidarity in the present.

Of course I did decide to change my style and to assume what is known these days as a "low profile." I vowed that I would head nothing, except my own business; that I would use my talents, as occasion came, to reinforce the initiative of others; that I would avoid public exposure as a "crusader" for justice and liberty, but rather "work behind the scenes."

On the whole that has worked. There was one notable exception, which very much involved your mother and doubtless would have involved you had you not been in the hospital. Your mother was responsible, you know, for calling the very gifted Cockerham sisters to the attention of Oldfields School in Maryland, which she had attended some years back. The school had never had black students before, and these two young parishioners seemed the right ones to be the first since they possessed superb intellects as well as all the middle-class social graces. Both seemed to establish themselves on the campus quickly; each newsletter from the school would bring fresh word of accomplishments or recognitions of Karen and Antoinette. And then it all went sour.

I suppose we will never know the precise details. As far as we could piece the story together, the girls fell into conversation with an unidentified stranger on the train back to school Christmas vacation 1968. When he learned where they were going, he told them that he was considering Oldfields for his daughter and wondered what they thought of the school. They proceeded to tell him! On the whole, they liked the school; but they did feel lonely, being the only black students, and they felt that they were popular and accepted only so long as they adopted the life style of the majority. Antoinette, the younger, said she did not intend to return once her sister graduated the following spring.

Apparently this conversation was reported to the headmaster. A few weeks later the girls were summoned to his office and told that he had decided to concur in their expressed desire to leave the school. They argued with him and said it was silly for them to leave at that point, since the year would soon be over. A few days later they were summoned again and informed they were to pack hand luggage immediately and leave on the next train for New York. They arrived in the city, penniless, and called their father to come for them at the station; they had been home several hours before a telegram arrived advising their parents of their "dismissal with cause."

The headmaster consistently refused to talk with the parents on the telephone. When I returned from a trip to Paris and was apprised of this situation, I called the headmaster and suggested, since the Schoonover family had been instrumental in placing the Cockerham girls at Oldfields initially, that we were due an explanation for this precipitous and extreme action. I was told that "the girls said they wanted to go home, and I said that they could go." I asked if it were his practice to deal with all adolescent complaints in the same fashion, and was assured that he always tried to let the girls do as they desired. I expressed skepticism that he really ran his school like that and said that if I were not leaving on another business trip the next morning, I would come to Maryland and insist on seeing him for a first-hand accounting of the affair. I was promised an invitation in writing to visit the school two weeks later and assured that I could talk with anyone I wished (although he was hesitant about letting me talk to Karen's and Antoinette's classmates because I might "upset" them). The invitation never came, and when an unpleasant confrontation took place a few weeks later on the Oldfields campus, the excuse given was that by then the Cockerham family had retained Bill Stringfellow as legal counsel and it was "assumed" that he also represented me.

Repeated pleas to the school to allow Karen at least to complete her semester's work so that admission to college might not be compromised were dismissed. No additional explanation of the school's action was provided to anyone, although some veiled references to the girls' "militance" were made. The headmaster had his telephone changed to an unlisted number so that he might be insulated against the rising tide of protest which was building in New York. Socially prominent parents or friends of the girls' classmates expressed sympathy to the outraged Cockerham family, but the executive of a large foundation basically expressed their attitudes when he urged the girls' mother not to fight back against this injustice "just for personal satisfaction."

But the family did want to fight back; and there were real militants in the wings willing to compound the injustice with violence. The Cockerham's dilemma was how to defend their children's future. To make no protest at all was unthinkable; to sanction vengeance of a violent nature was equally impossible.

All this was very hard for your mother, as well. She had loved Oldfields School. "Recommending the Cockerham girls is the only good thing I ever did for the school," she would say. She did not want anything to happen which might damage the reputation of the school. But even more important, she did not want anything to happen to damage the future of the Cockerham girls and the close relationship which had developed between our two families through the years.

After a lot of thought, we decided to offer to charter a bus to take the Cockerhams and many of their friends to Oldfields on graduation day. The plan was to make one more plea, as dramatically as we could, that Karen be graduated with her class. If that failed, it was agreed that we would interrupt the graduation exercise and make our own recognition of Karen. The entire group expressed its willingness to be jailed, if necessary, in order to carry out this plan.

It was a beautiful day in May, 1969. The graduating girls were beautifully gowned in long white dresses and each carried a bouquet of spring flowers. One of the first to see us shouted in disbelief, "My God, the Cockerhams are here." Immediately many of the girls clustered around Karen; some began to share their flowers with her so that she, too, soon had a bouquet. A few of us sought out the headmaster to make our plea. In turn we were referred to the urbane Wall Street lawyer who is chairman of the school's board of trustees. Our request was denied. He suggested that we were making too much of the matter. When we advised him that recognition would be given to Karen that day whether he liked it or not, he graciously said that we were welcome to stay as "spectators."

The girls began to process and to take their places around the May Queen. Karen, her father and I, and about fifteen grim-faced men joined the procession. Soon someone whispered to us that we were in the wrong line, and so we joined another procession made up of seniors. Karen—rather short and stout, in colorful daishiki—contrasted clearly with the slim, blonde girls in white all around her. Once everyone was in position, the girls moved in pairs to present their flowers to the May Queen. Then something happened that we had not counted on. About a third of the way through this ceremony, a girl suddenly diverged from the march and presented her flowers to Karen. Others began to do the same, some giving her all they had, some giving her a part before going on to the May Queen. Her mother stood next to a shade tree and wept, although a letter sent by the school to alumni later said that throughout Mrs. Cockerham had been going from girl to girl demanding that they present their flowers to her daughter. It is well known, of course, that an outrageous lie may more readily be believed than a plausible lie.

Then the names of the graduates were called and each girl moved out of the line to collect her diploma. Traditionally the names had been called in alphabetical order, and our plan had been to interrupt this ceremony at the point when Karen's name should be called; but this time the names were called in random order. Again someone whispered to us how many graduates there were to be, and as soon as the last name was called I burst into the center of the grassy field where all this was taking place and called Karen's name. My speech was totally *ad lib* and I don't remember all that I said. Essentially, however, it said that in days to come

Karen would achieve honors which some schools would undoubtedly want to claim even though they had no right to do so. I went on to say that even though Oldfields did not choose to recognize her previous accomplishments, a large group of her friends and family were there to express their solidarity, their pride, their affection, and their hope. And then it was all over, and soon we got back on the bus for the return trip.

Oldfields got a tremendous amount of unwanted national publicity because of that event. The press was told that the matter of Karen's diploma would be decided by the faculty at a meeting the following week. Documented reports came quickly about the firing of the assistant headmaster, who had been quoted by some reporters as supporting the legitimacy of the Cockerham's grievances. Finally a letter came proposing that the diploma be given *in absentia* after Karen had successfully completed a semester at some recognized college. A whole year has passed, and Karen has once again demonstrated her superior scholarship at Middlebury, but Oldfields has taken no step to make any kind of amends.

Instead the school has chosen to defend itself in lengthy letters to alumni largely by telling falsehoods about the Cockerhams. Interestingly enough, although presumably still a *bona fide* graduate of the school, your mother was dropped from the Oldfields mailing list until just recently. The saddest part of the saga, for me, has been the willingness of Mummy's friends and classmates at Oldfields to assume that the Cockerham girls must have done something to warrant expulsion. It is just inconceivable to them that an establishmentarian-type institution could ever be guilty of cruelty and crudeness. I have retold this story in such detail, Polly, because I wanted to say that we stick with East Harlem and refuse to break fellowship with our brothers there because actions like those of Oldfields are still normative for American society and some of us have to have guts enough to label it for the immorality it is. And we have to do it even if you can never go to Oldfields—it would be over my dead body, anyway—and even if no one is grateful for what we have done. One does not need gratitude for doing what is right.

I guess what I am saying is that what a man finds especially liberating is to act with integrity. It is assumed by most people that everyone's primary responsibility is to protect himself, to act out of self-interest, to trample if he can on those who are weaker or less astute. And that is precisely why the world is in such a mess.

People like us, Polly, never have any security. No one really has, but most people can prolong the illusion that they have. Catastrophe is always imminent for us. No matter how prudent and cautious and self-protective we are, we have no immunity against injury and pain and death. It is not even a reasonable option for us to withdraw from society to gain relative safety. Our bones can break almost as easily in the protection of home as on the street. Whatever tiny margin of safety can be gained through such draconian measures is bought at the price of living death. As Dr. Wilson once said to me, "There are worse things than broken legs."

In a funny kind of way we find our lives only by throwing them away, by taking all kinds of stupid risks not only to physical well-being but also to any self-centered notion that we can somehow be independent of other men. What I have been saying to you in these letters is that I have found my life through the acceptance of those risks, especially the risk of entrusting my life to encounter with all kinds of human beings. People marvel at my "independence," completely failing to see that my independence is a by-product of acknowledged interdependence. I have achieved freedom to give what I have because I have been willing to affirm how much others have given.

The willingness to be open, to trust, to approach

others in freedom is perhaps a great contribution we can make to the world, Polly. Oh, I know, it is very hard to live like that. Sometimes the temptations are overpowering. The only way it is possible is to receive that constant "transfusion of grace" which, as I have said over and over in these letters, has come to us both when we least expected it and then from the most unlikely sources.

In that, I suppose, our experience parallels that of Jesus of Nazareth. Not only do I think his "style of life" is the only one I can rationally defend. More than that, his final victory over evil and suffering and death gives me hope that we—and all men—can and shall reach the "kingdom." There the physical burdens will be laid aside, and the walls of separation between human beings shall be torn down, and we shall all be free to love and live as God always intended us to do.

Good night, my beloved Polly.

Daddy

Postscript

Dear Polly,

Since this book was published more than thirty years ago, much has happened. To bring the story up to date, after being at New York Theological Seminary for ten years I returned to my "first love" as pastor of Central Baptist Church in Wayne, Pennsylvania, where I stayed until 1983. That year I came to Florida to found a theological seminary. Florida Center for Theological Studies is now a thriving, fully accredited school with a multicultural, multidenominational, multiethnic student body, faculty, and board of directors. As my health deteriorated dangerously, I retired in 1994. I am now an old man, beset by all kinds of physical problems, increasingly restricted in range of activities.

You, on the other hand, are a vibrant young woman in midlife with a significant history of accomplishment. So this will be an attempt to summarize what has happened to you since the book first appeared.

When your two years at St. Hilda's and St. Hugh's ended, we approached Dalton School on Manhattan's upper east side. It was a large school, will all grades, and they willingly accepted you. It was a secular bastion greatly influenced by the philosophy of John Dewey, yet in some respects more "religious" than the schools you had already attended. You were there for eight years.

Several times you had fractures that caused you to miss weeks of classes. They would send homework to the hospital and your exams were monitored at the special public elementary school at Special Surgery. Some Dalton instructors even came to the hospital to tutor you.

You did well there, but frustrated by your inability to socialize with your peers who came and went freely. Because we could not afford taxis, your mother walked you to and from school. You were self-conscious about having to be picked up—"It made me feel like a little kid," you told me years later.

One summer we visited friends at Northfield/Mt. Hermon Schools—a very old and good boarding school in Massachusetts. Their daughter, a student, showed you around, and you said wistfully that you wished you could go there, too. But the buildings were old, had steps everywhere with no elevators, and the winters were full of snow. Still our friends sought for a school that might be more compatible. One in Connecticut seemed more promising, but when we visited the headmaster blurted out, in your presence, "Your daughter is unacceptable." Inquiries at other schools in the Northeast were no more promising. But your desire grew.

Finally, realizing there had to be an agency that could help, your mother found a listing in the telephone directory for The Private Schools Advisory Service. They were most responsive and said they could think of a few schools that they were willing to approach. "If they are interested," we were told, "they will call you."

That same day Walter "Judge" Mason, director of admissions at Verde Valley School in Sedona, Arizona, visited PSAS. He said they had never had a handicapped student but were willing to consider it. In the summers they ran a camp for children with muscular dystrophy, lining the paths with window screens (later known as "Polly paths")! This small school in the gorgeous Red Rocks area of northern Arizona invited us to come for a visit.

You loved the school as soon as you saw it. While your parents talked with officials about tuition, fees, and scholarships, you were off for interviews with student members of the admissions committee. Everyone felt it would work.

We drove you there and got you settled. Your "brother" Brad Rentzel flew out to help us drive back. As we drove away from your dorm, you sat in the entrance with tears running down your face. Your mother was sobbing in the back seat.

You were involved in several days of off-campus orientation, so we could not call you until we got home. You wanted to be independent, but you didn't know how. So when we did reach you, you cried out, "I've made a terrible mistake! Come back for me." I told you to stick it out, that it would get easier.

But it didn't. You even deliberately fell out of your chair, although you didn't hurt yourself. But in a few weeks you did fall, and you bent the rod in your femur. The small-town orthopedist told you he had never done a rodding, "but I sure would like to try!" "Daddy, can I come home and go see Dr. Wilson?" Of course I said yes. But, I added, "When you recover, you have to return to Verde Valley." When you flew back you announced defiantly, "Yes, I know I have to go back." As your recovery proceeded, you changed your mind and said you wanted to graduate from Dalton. We argued, but finally took you to see the headmaster. He wisely reminded you that you had promised Verde Valley you would return, and felt you should keep your promise. He would keep in touch with the other school, and if both agreed down the road that it would be better for you to return to Dalton, he would approve.

So you went back for two months and started crossing days off the calendar. We called you to say that Verde Valley had sent us a contract for the next year that had to be returned with a deposit. "What shall we do?" "Give me a couple of days and I will call you," you said.

You did call and said, "Send the check." What had changed your mind? "Ditch day" had come along—the day the students would all call in sick. They wouldn't let you stay in the dorm. The boys carried your chair down the hill toward Oak Creek where they were going swimming. Then you got out and inched your way over rocks and tree roots. Someone lent you a t-shirt, and another cut-off jeans. So you went swimming, too. "It was the first time I felt included, that I belonged," you told us. Now you were having fun! Even though you fell off the ramp later in the year and had to have a cast, everything went well.

During spring break your senior year; you came to Pennsylvania to go with us to Wayne were I was being installed as pastor of Central Baptist Church. A few miles from Wayne, on the Pennsylvania Turnpike, a tractor trailer jackknifed and broadsided the driver side of my car. You rebroke your arm and I had a broken femur. We were taken to the nearest hospital where we called Dr. Wilson, who said we should return to New York by ambulance.

I learned years later how traumatic that had been for you. "I didn't want to get out of the car. I wanted to stay with you." Until then, you had seen your father as indestructible.

After getting a new cast, you returned to Arizona and graduated a few weeks later. Your mother and I came out to applaud and cheer! I gave the invocation—that's what fathers who are ministers do!

You had applied to six colleges and were accepted by five (Georgetown, your first choice, turned you down). You elected to go to Boston University, as it was the best academically. This transition was easy. You quickly made friends and enjoyed being in Boston. The chief problem was that you had to have surgery on your left arm (there were seven surgeries altogether, as I remember), so you wore a cast almost the entire time you were in school. You graduated in 1982 with a degree in sociology.

You applied only to the graduate school in social work at University of Southern California and were accepted. We drove you to Pasadena, bought you a car, rented an apartment, and set up a bank account with the proceeds from the

Pennsylvania accident insurance settlement. No tears this time as we left you!

After a couple of months you dropped out of USC—not what you were looking for. A few years later you took some courses at San Diego toward a master's in public health, but never had time to finish it. Working full-time and going to school part-time did not mix.

While at Boston University you called me one day to say you had decided to be baptized and confirmed as an Episcopalian. ("I am the product of a mixed marriage," you used to say—"half Baptist and half Episcopalian. And neither half liked to go to church!")

Just then, the telephone went dead and neither of us could reestablish the connection. The next morning, you told your mother you feared I had hung up on you because I was infuriated at your decision. ("Will Daddy have to give up his church?") When we finally connected, I assured you that I was delighted, that I would have supported your decision whatever it had been.

Your baptism/confirmation took place a few weeks later at St. Paul's Cathedral where John Coburn, an old friend, was bishop of Massachusetts. It was also where your mother had been confirmed many years before.

It was a wonderful occasion—very ecumenical. In the absence of your Episcopal godmother and godfather (from the elaborate service of infant dedication at my church in East Harlem in 1960), a Roman Catholic college classmate and Fr. Christopher Keenan, a Franciscan Friar in brown habit and cincture (a former student of mine from New York), represented them. I read the Old Testament lesson.

That was the beginning of what remains a serious commitment to the church. When you moved to Pasadena, you visited—a courtesy to me—an American Baptist Church; but soon gravitated to All Saints Episcopal Church, which still has a special place in your heart. At this huge congregation—one that could be characterized as a "megachurch"—you found not only a place of welcome but also of service. You were an usher some Sundays, occasionally taught Sunday School, served on various committees and taskforces, and for a long time you proofread the elaborate order of service in which the text of prayers, hymns, scriptures, and activities were printed.

When you moved to San Diego, you joined a much smaller parish where you were eventually elected to the vestry. A new rector objected to your outspoken advocacy of causes that were not hers and finally marginalized your participation.

Then you went to see Dean John Chane at St. Paul's Cathedral. You liked each other immediately and he worked at finding ways of utilizing your interests and skills. You are still happily a member there, even though John Chane has gone on to become the Bishop of Washington.

In all this you have followed your parents' commitments to justice and peace issues.

After dropping out of USC, you began to look for a job. Because of your physical circumstances, there weren't many things you could do. No one would hire you even to be a cashier.

Your first paying job was to read to a blind student at Fuller Seminary, struggling with the pronunciation of theological words you could not define. You were paid minimum wage with no benefits.

You answered an ad in the *Los Angeles Times* for a study at USC Medical School, that involved interviews in the field. The person who interviewed you felt you were not mobile enough to handle the job. She was, however, so impressed with you that she persuaded another doctor to consider you for a study involving telephone interviews with parents of children diagnosed as having bone cancer, who enrolled in a study through the Children's Cancer Study Group. You did that for three years for $900 a month plus benefits!

Getting bored with this, you responded to another ad in 1987 for a coordinator position in another cancer study at Children's Hospital Los Angeles. You asked a nurse related to the previous study for a reference and she called Dr. Daniel Hays to urge that you be considered. You had two interviews with the noted doctor heading up the study and were offered the job. That's when you first met John Landsverk, who has played an important role in your life and career ever since. Now your salary was to be $11 an hour.

For the next four years you helped organize the study, wrote reports, and presented portions of the data at meetings. It was too large for CHLA to do the study alone and the National Cancer Institutes of the National Institutes of Health, which provided the funding, wanted you to do it collaboratively with a well-known group in Boston (one that you considered to be inept). You were sent to see them and get them to "shape up," but they treated you as an inferior and said they would produce the required data. You returned to Los Angeles and recommended to Dr. Hays that they should be "fired" and that a solid but less prestigious group in Columbus be substituted. That was the group Dr. Hays had originally wanted.

The National Cancer Institutes called everyone together in Washington for an accounting. John felt you should go, too. When the question was raised about the sources of the population you were studying, you were asked to make the presentation. You explained that you had taken every case in your files, and if you had no current information you diligently sought to find it by using telephone directories, death registries, auto registrations, and whatever other sources you could think of. Boston, on the other hand, had gone only to their out-of-date patient files, thus producing a much smaller number. NIH was so impressed by your performance; they terminated Boston and approved the affiliation with Columbus.

After the meeting the director from NIH asked you, "Where did you get your PhD?"

When the study finished, you helped write a proposal for the California Division of the American Cancer Society on dating and marriage among childhood cancer survivors.

You were encouraged by John to consider getting your MPH degree at San Diego State and he arranged an office for you at Children's Hospital San Diego. When the ACS study ended, you got a job as research secretary in the orthopedic department of Scipps Clinic in La Jolla.

Then something happened that changed your life drastically and, perhaps, permanently. While crossing the parking lot of your supermarket, you were struck by a speeding jeep and catapulted out of your chair. You fractured your sacrum and coccyx. You were in such pain and missed so much work that you voluntarily terminated your job. Out of work for a year, you survived on the insurance settlement your attorney negotiated. You are still suffering the effects of that injury even now.

When you were finally ready to go back to work, you were offered a half-time position back at Children's Hospital Los Angeles coordinating their participation in a nationwide study on the health status of long-term cancer survivors. That meant that you had to commute again.

Back in San Diego you found another half-time job recruiting people for clinical trials for an endocrinologist in private practice.

Soon the cancer survivors' study was expanded, so they could offer you a full-time job for fifteen months. This time you moved back to L.A. At the end of that, you were cut back to half-time. So it was back to San Diego where you returned to the clinical trials job fulltime, only to get fired nine months later because your computer skills were poor. (You assure me they are much improved now!)

During this time, you developed severe shoulder pain and had to go on disability while your shoulders were reconstructed.

After that you found a part-time (later extended to a full-time) job doing a study for the Naval Hospital on postpartum weight loss, but there were no benefits.

In August 1997, John Landsverk left you a message saying he needed you for a new telephone interviewing position at Children's Hospital San Diego ("You are the best interviewer I have ever known!"). It would include questionnaire development, recruitment of subjects, tracking—in other words, all the things you excel at! You have been doing that for nine years now—a job record!

Recently you reached the top of the pay scale for this job, so they reclassified your job as "research specialist" so you can continue to get annual increases. No longer are you involved with childhood cancer but now focus on child and adolescent mental health systems and interview agency staff, both government and private.

You inherited a love of travel from your parents. You took many trips with us across the country, to Europe, and to the Caribbean. In recent years you have been on another trip to Europe, one to Hawaii, and a cruise to Alaska with your mother, as well as a Caribbean cruise with both of us. You and your mother also have done a couple of automobile trips in the Northeast in recent years. There have been occasional trips related to your work. Wherever you go, you manage to route yourself so that you can see various friends.

But the most major trips you have taken on your own. While at San Diego State you met Wendy, who became your "best friend." In your visits to see Wendy, now married to an American diplomat, you have been to Ecuador twice, to Paraguay twice, and to Rome last year. During this trip you went to an appearance by Pope Benedict, shook his hand, was blessed by him, and had your picture taken with him. A return trip is planned by 2007.

Now that my traveling days are over, I am very jealous!

Finally, a few comments about your health. Especially since the Jeep accident you have been in the hospital many times, having surgery on your shoulders as well as your hips. You have found wonderful doctors who take good care of you and also to care for you as a person. Occasionally you miss days of work from your job or have to do much of your telephoning from home. You could not ask for more understanding employers; you never seem to run out of "sick time." But then, you are the best interviewer they have every seen!

Your mother and I worry about your health but are no longer able to go to California to help you. Rather, you worry more and more about us and make fairly frequent trips to Florida to help us. Last year you spent several weeks here with you mother when I was gravely ill.

We talk several times a week usually, and none of us hesitates to call to encourage and inform. We are a very close-knit family. Your mother and I are very proud of you, Polly. You are a great person.

                        Love,

                            Dad

Afterword

Polly was asked to hang a portrait of her father among several portraits at St. Paul's Cathedral and to write a message to accompany it. This is what she wrote:

> "My father has always been my best teacher. He's taught me that having a 'disability' is like having brown hair—it doesn't define who I am. Whenever less was expected of me because of using a wheelchair, he always expected more. Whenever I was told that I couldn't do something or go somewhere because I might break a bone, he always encouraged me to take a risk. Thank you, Dad, for always believing in me and for pushing me to be the best 'disabled' person I can be."

www.ingramcontent.com/pod-product-compliance
Lightning Source LLC
Chambersburg PA
CBHW070633220426
R18178600001B/R181786PG43193CBX00026B/41